ILLUSION IN LOVING

A Psychoanalytic Approach to the Evolution of Intimacy and Autonomy

Joel Shor

and

Jean Sanville

Double Helix Press
Los Angeles

Jean Sanville is currently serving as Dean of the Institute for Clinical Social Work, and is on the Faculty of the Institute of the Los Angeles Society for Psychoanalytic Psychology. She is past president of the California Society for Clinical Social Work, and has been on the Faculty of the School of Social Welfare at U.C.L.A. since 1948. She has been in private practice since 1958.

Joel Shor is on the Faculty and a Training Analyst of the Institute of the Los Angeles Society for Psychoanalytic Psychology. He has been on the Faculty of the University of Southern California Law Center and Yale University Department of Psychiatry, as well as of New York University, Sarah Lawrence College, Tavistock Clinic, London, and a Rockefeller Foundation Fellow in the Humanities. In private practice since 1948.

ISBN: 0-930578-00-7
Library of Congress Catalog Card Number: 77-85416

Printed in the United States of America

Double Helix Press
1300 Tigertail Road Los Angeles, California 90049

From our parents and teachers,

for our children and students,

to our colleagues,

and to one another

Table of Contents

Prelude to a Primary Illusion

A quality of chaos appears to permeate the realms of private and public relationship today. The current cultural climate of permissiveness is drastically modifying the manners and morals of love and sex. Two seemingly contradictory trends are flourishing among both men and women: an inclination toward instant intimacy and simultaneously toward narcissistic self-centeredness. Expressions of closeness which until recently signified a depth and duration of familiarity and commitment now are offered easily and accepted or rejected casually. No promises of love or of continuity are initially given or expected; explicit disavowals of deep or permanent feelings are considered as protection for the still private individualities. Each person also claims and proclaims the need, the wish, and the right to be apart and alone, and to pursue separate interests and goals, serious or whimsical. The co-existence of both forms of indulgence, in connectedness and in autonomy, can be confounding to both the moralistic pessimists and the innocent optimists amongst us. When is the chaos malignant and when may it be benign?

Even our various professions of scientific psychotherapy are having difficulties attending to and understanding these new human data without bias. Yet this very co-existence of two seemingly opposed dimensions, instant intimacy and automatic autonomy, may contain vital cues about next phases in the evolution of human loving.

In the changing social atmosphere, the clinical psychotherapist can observe details of the sexual revolution as it is explored and exploited for still hidden hopes and wishes. We see substantial indications that women are leading men toward a fuller experience of a romantic illusion of perfect loving. We believe that an illusion was always embedded in human intimacy, that it is now re-emerging as women and men learn to enjoy more flexible sharing of traditional male and female roles and functions, and that it is revitalizing the search for new dimensions of mutuality and individuality.

Literary and historical studies are discovering earlier phases of the movement for women's liberation, even before the nineteenth century. The old courtly romantic spirit had been suppressed by rationalistic judgments and puritanical threats. The pressures of Victorian morality provoked a new and deeper protest. Then, both open-ended democracy and Darwinism evolved. A fresh spirit of aggressive individualism began to permeate Western culture, and the new self-assertiveness led to a popular vision of personal fulfillment through perfect love. Since World War I, we have seen a further thrust toward sexual freedoms, and the surge continues to spiral.

We note the widespread humanistic movement today, with growth centers and encounter groups attracting youth and adults explicitly seeking both better love experiences and expanding self-development. The new slogans emphasize "here and now" and "let it all hang out" attitudes, as well as an open attention to bodily sensations for finding flowing sensuality. Can the clinician attend to and understand these new human data without bias? And if so, what can he/she say about current and next phases in the further evolution of human individuality and intimacy?

It is our thesis that a definable dialectic ideal is inherent in the human hope to experience fulfillment in love. We see this vision as an "illusion" intrinsic to the deepest impetus for every intimate relationship from infancy to dying. We believe that social progress is propelled by the increasing power of this persistent and ineradicable wish. We work clinically to help our clients discover the secret wellsprings of this hope and to undo the unrealistic defensive fears, anxieties and hostilities which are constraining their fuller experience of this illusion of perfect intimacy. Our aim here is to develop this hypothesis by reporting our clinical approach to and observations on these processes as people reach for the potentialities and react to the personal impacts of liberation movements among women—and men—today.

The traditional romantic dream stressed a state of intense and turgid binding between two aching and yearning spirits. Prior to this passionate closure there stretched a continuously painful period of private struggle and search for the one perfect partner; and following the consummation there was to be a profound relief and a peace that was claimed as eternal protection against any new hunger or aloneness. The core hope was for a final solution that would make unnecessary any more separateness, or any further expansion of the relationship or modification of oneself. Thus the image of happiness was a static one, not dialectic. This traditional model has not been able to survive among reasonable people cognizant of ongoing human evolution and of open-ended individual development.

The new vision of romantic fulfillment is a more complex image. It contains two seemingly contrary qualities of feeling: occasions of absolute unity with one another in perfectly harmonious identity, and times of completely self-centered spontaneity enjoyed in trusting innocence and self-confidence. Although not always on a conscious level, each person wishes to experience a smoothly flowing oscillation between these two states without strain, pain or contradiction, with no concern about domination or exploitation, power or submission; with no shame or guilt; with no conflict felt between loving and privacy, between sharing and selfishness. These dreams can be glimpsed if a spirit of flexible playfulness permeates both the sense of self and the relationship with the other.

Throughout human history, doctrines and dogmas about human nature have emphasized either the socially cooperative or the individually competitive aspect of our double-headed hypothesis. Warnings and wisdoms have been pronounced about adhering to one position or to the other. We see such recurrent one-sidedness in the historical parade of ideologies, literary, medical, philosophical, political and religious, formulated for human happiness. Even the scientific psychologists and psychoanalysts characterize their positions as "object-relations theory" or as "ego psychology," thus stressing a predominant importance either of the human relationship or of the sense of a separate self.

Our approach presumes an initial coexistence of both dimensions of experience in the human infant. Inevitably, imperfections will be felt as insufficiencies and intrusions into this primary condition; and these disruptions of the moments of easy flowing original bliss propel the subsequent stages of human development, social and individual. The larger assumption is that the original dream, with its dual aspects, becomes anchored in each person's neural system and continues to provide both the model and the impetus for further fulfillment. Later editions of human loving may incorporate and integrate the awareness and the capacities gained during intermediary phases of growth. We will describe how ongoing maturing permits an ever richer mutuality, moving dialectically toward adult versions of the primary illusion.

Early in our training for our work as psychoanalytic therapists, we found classical cues towards our thesis. Freud wrote (1908) for "Civilized Sexual Morality":

> Fear of the consequences of sexual intercourse first bring the married couple's physical affection to an end; and then, as a remoter result, it usually puts a stop as well to the mental sympathy between them, which should have been the successor to their original passionate love. The spiritual disillusionment and bodily deprivation to which most marriages are thus doomed puts both partners back in the state they were in before their marriage, except for being the poorer by the loss of an illusion . . .

The word "illusion" has been defined in quite contrary ways; it derives from the Latin *in ludere* which can be translated either as "in play" or "against play." More popularly, pejorative meanings prevail, such as "error," "fallacy of vision," "insubstantiality," even "delusion" or "hallucination." Psychotherapists often explicitly aim to rid the psyche of all illusions and they deem the wish for fusion pathological. These negative definitions assume that our judgments and decisions can and must always be based on solid and sufficient knowledge of reality, of the good and the truth in every act of decision and every decision to act.

Freud has suggested that the ongoing evolution of our sciences and the uncontrolled imperfections in our methods of observation should encourage a more open attitude toward beliefs, especially about the complexities of subjective experience. In his speculations about *The Future of an Illusion,* he proposes that:

> Illusions need not necessarily be false—that is to say unrealizable or in contradiction to reality . . . Thus we call a belief an illusion when a wish-fulfillment is a prominent factor in its motivation, and in doing so we disregard its relation to reality, just as the illusion itself sets no store by verification.

Yet he also recognizes dangerous illusions:

> Must not the assumptions that determine our political regulations be called illusions as well? And is it not the case that in our civilization the relations between the sexes are disturbed by an erotic illusion or by a number of such illusions?

Among these negative images, he had previously identified the compelling stereotypes of the heroic leader and the omnipotent authority in social movements, and models of the precious virgin and the sensual harlot in sexual relating. All of these images are seen as one-sided idealizations, and therefore as oppressive, belittling and pathogenic for the person. Much of Freud's clinical and sociological work explores the malignant, rather than benign functioning of illusions. There is one crucial exception, the psychoanalytic transference processes, in which the analyst helps the patient to transform his magical and monstrous perceptions and feelings about the analyst, and about himself, into benign reparative experiences.

Although it cannot be claimed that Freud's writings dealt much with the significance of play or of mutuality in adult maturity, he did describe how the transference can create "a playground, . . . an intermediate region between illness and real life through which the transition from the one to the other is made" (1914a). He saw this process as "a piece of real experience made possible by especially favorable conditions," essentially depending on the therapist's setting up this playground where the patient could explore "in almost complete freedom" the pathogenic forces within him.

Freud here identified transference interpretation as "the main instrument" in his method, and then declared that any therapy which takes it as its starting point "has a right to call itself psycho-analysis, even though it arrives at results other than my own" (1914).

We do arrive at results other than his (Freud, 1931, 1932), since many social-evolutionary forces have revised the human data. But we see the principles of transference analysis as Freud's most significant and lasting contribution to the understanding and further evolution of the human condition. Effective playing of this "instrument" requires a special "safe-space" in which the patient can express, explore and repair feelings and fantasies of primitive pains and anxieties. In this clinical approach, the emphasis on the patient's sense of psychic freedom is crucial; we will attempt to demonstrate its workings and its advantages over the widely popular humanistic, existential and behavioristic methods.

People are reaching for new forms of wish fulfillment, new qualities of hope, new depths of illusion. In this book we will describe the fresh complaints we hear from those who come for professional help, and the private gropings that emerge from these new feelings of protest. Our patients range from the paralyzed through the psychopathic, from those who anticipate complications in their lives and proceed cautiously, to others who act first and confront predicaments later. When we work well, they come to measure their own failures and successes, and move to new confidence and new efforts in rearranging their resources and relationships. Our major contribution is a way of listening and of offering our best tentative interpretations of hidden wishes for elemental fulfillment of the primary illusion behind their anxious and defensive behaviors in our presence, as seen in their transference projections.

The main processes and results of these clinical dialogues are the essential content of this book. We do not pretend to know how typical or how selective are the people we have studied. Of course, any personal data which might reveal the identity of patients have been disguised.

The frequent use of "we" and "our" throughout the book is a natural expression of the shared authorship. Jean Sanville has participated for over five years in the formulations being presented, and the listing of references records her separate and our joint writings which are woven into major sections of the text. Her many-levelled involvement in the basic conceptions and their clinical implications literally permeates this work. Since our separate identities have not been completely abandoned, there is a resulting fluctuation in style throughout the book. Obviously, the double spiral continues to evolve; we are of course planning to test, refine and revise the ideas presented here both conjointly and independently. The speculative Postlude foreshadows some wider lines of interest to us.

To facilitate the further development of these theories, we have reprinted in the Appendix two recent papers, on the theory of sexual development and on the theory of therapy, both as extensions of the essential notions in the main body of the book. Thus we hope our colleagues may come to consider the new human data in terms of our evolutionary social perspective, and consequently to review their methods and theories for offering professional help. At the same time, we wish to share with a wider audience the inner experience of our working to understand and to meet the fresh complaints of our clients as they reach for better editions of the primary illusion.

Our thanks to the professional journals, especially to *The Psychoanalytic Review* and *The Clinical Social Work Journal* for permission for the use of some of our previous publications. Also, our special gratitude to Marilyn Morgan-Hamilton, Master Analyst, The Guild for Psychoanalysis, New York City, to Ruth L. Optner, author, *Writing From the Inside Out* (Harper & Row, New York, 1977), and to Christopher D. Stone, Professor of Law, U.S.C., for their very helpful suggestions and editing. We feel most indebted to our patients, whose courage and confidences are evoking the data and the cues to further new ideas and spirits for the human experience.

Joel Shor

Interlude on the Persistence of Illusion

According to Plato's Symposium, the sexes were originally not two as they are now but three: man, woman and the union of the two, the androgynes. These latter beings were mighty and strong, and the "thoughts of their hearts" were so great that the gods felt threatened by their insolence. Zeus at first thought to annihilate them all together but, exercising a degree of restraint, he retaliated against their hubris by cutting them in two.

From then on the two parts of human beings, each desiring his (or her) other half, "came together, and throwing their arms about one another, entwined in mutual embrace, longing to grow into one; they were on the point of dying from hunger and self neglect, because they did not like to do anything apart." In pity, Zeus invented for them a new plan: he turned the parts of generation around to the front . . . "and they sowed their seed no longer like grasshoppers in the ground, but in one another, thus continuing the race. . . . so ancient is the desire for one another planted in us."

The Symposium goes on to describe that "when one of them meets with his other half, the actual half of himself . . . the pair are lost in an amazement of love and friendship and intimacy. . . . these are the people who pass their whole lives together." Yet, Plato adds, "they could not explain what they desire of one another." Plato himself ponders it, saying, "for the intense yearning which each of them has toward the other does not appear to be [only] the desire of lovers' intercourse, but of something else which the soul of either evidently desires and cannot tell and of which he has only a dark and doubtful presentiment."

Disenchantment with Marriage

On today's scene there are fewer and fewer couples who pass all of their lives together, and those who stay with each other often appear to be living lives of quiet, or not so quiet, desperation rather than of delight in each other's company. Yet those who separate and divorce do quite regularly, like the characters in Plato's myths keep seeking new mates and attempting again and again to unite with them in the hope of being thus completed and fulfilled. Even those cynics who are impressed both with the overwhelming odds against relationships being lasting and with their own and their friends' failures in love, even they tend to harbor deep within a phantasy that somewhere, someday, somehow they will find the one with whom they might attain perfect concord.

Still there is heard loudly pronounced a disillusion with marriage, and from a clinical point of view it is not difficult to see how this came about. In the past we projected on to the institution of marriage all our dreams of self-repair. Our parents were imperfect, imperfectly reared us. We were left with mistrusts, doubts and shames, angers and guilts, feelings of inferiority and inadequacy. But we looked to marriage as to a healer; it was to be our salvation. Specifically, the chosen spouse was to be all that the former caretakers and mentors had failed to be, and such perfection would of course cure all our deficits and perfect us. On an unconscious level, we took with utmost seriousness the myths that we would marry and live happily ever after.

With such high hopes and elaborate expectations it is no wonder that we set ourselves up for the inevitable fall, for disappointment in relationships and despair about ourselves. And no wonder too that we have turned upon marriage as we once turned upon our parents, with outrage. That to which we looked as the source of goodness and restoration, capable of rendering us whole and sound, has instead, like the parents, failed us, left us feeling still bad, still flawed.

And so we claim to have repudiated marriage itself, denouncing it as a no longer viable social institution, perhaps just as in adolescence we repudiated our parents and declared loudly that we no longer needed or wanted them. Yet, just as our renunciation of parents was not total, so our renunciation of marriage is also partial. We attempt to modify various aspects of the traditional model to make it serve us better, and we experiment with new models of togetherness, more tentative in nature, allowing for less complicated egress should they be untenable. But these alternative models are often viewed, consciously or unconsciously, as practice for the real thing, rehearsals for the main event—ultimate marriage.

Disappointment With Psychotherapy

As there has been disillusion with marriage, so there has been disillusion with psychotherapy. Many have turned to the mental health professionals for repair, endowing them too with omnipotence and omniscience. Here also many have been disappointed, and perhaps most bitterly with psychoanalysis, precisely because it seemed to promise most. They submitted to its demands for a long term commitment, lying four or five scheduled hours a week on the couch, dutifully associating and remembering dreams, spending enormous sums over the two to ten years that it might take to "complete" the analysis. A considerable portion ended up dissatisfied with the results, feeling perhaps more knowledgeable about themselves, but not freer for the pursuit of that love for which they yearned. So psychoanalysis found itself denounced too, abandoned in favor of therapies which promised quick cures via simpler methods. Patients flocked to therapists practicing Gestalt, transactional analysis, various humanistic approaches, and behavioral methods. Although they often felt partial gratifications in each experience, many were still discontent, complaining of inability to hold onto the nice feelings, and they continued to seek. Often persons experimented with the whole gamut of newer therapies, little recognizing that each had covertly borrowed a piece of Freud's thinking and had blown it up into an allegedly total therapy.

While purporting to attend to the "here and now," most of these new treatment approaches ignored or distorted the concepts of transference and resistance which are at the heart of psychoanalytic method, concepts which can enable patient and therapist to deal with the past, not per se, but as existing in and exerting influence over the present. Ideally, through analysis of the irrational feelings projected onto the therapist, hangovers from old relationships with those in authority, the patient can be freed of obstacles to clearer perception of others, and hence of self. And through analysis of those forces which pressure him to resist the very changes he is asking, he can cease defeating himself in his aspirations to grow and unfold. Attention to transference and resistance lead to the basic ethic of psychoanalytically based therapies, respect for the patient's right to self-determination. Through declining the role of all-knowing and all-powerful authority, and through recognizing and strengthening the patient's inner resources, the therapist gives the patient back the capacity to direct his own life course.

Psychoanalytic therapists, trained to introspection about their processes and results, may be provoked by the present situation to engage in repair of their own theory and methods. They may come to separate the chaff, which is the ritual of prescribed couch and frequency and duration of sessions, from the wheat, the essence contained in the principle of honoring the patient's right and ability to determine for himself where he shall place himself in any given hour, how often and how long he will come, and indeed to ascertain for himself his changing aims and how and when he wants to reach for them.

It is our thesis that there has been a hidden bias in much traditional psychotherapeutic practice, a bias toward relationships, and a relative neglect of that line of development which is of the self (Shor, 1977). That bias has been a determining factor in the setting up of those prescriptive procedures just mentioned and has obfuscated the fact that these determinations, when made by the therapist, not freely chosen by the patient, do in fact reinforce the latter's expectation that he has only to be a "good patient" and the cure will follow. Hence he is justified if he complains, "I have done what you told me, but you have not delivered what I asked."

Thus both marriage and psychoanalytic therapy have seemed to promise that the answer to human loneliness and pain lies in a commitment to relationship. Neither, we believe, has sufficiently attended to the equal importance of the unfolding of self potentialities, which might lead to better results.

Renewal Of Hope

In spite of the disillusion with marriage, there is much evidence that it is still sought after, still seen, sometimes openly and again covertly, as the symbol of blissful, eternal togetherness. And in spite of the disillusion with psychoanalysis, there are indications that it is still seen as the therapy of therapies, offering open-ended possibilities for human fulfillment. The very failures of both come to be the impetus for repair, for further attempts to comprehend what has gone wrong and to invoke remedies.

Like Plato, we might wonder what it can be that the soul is desiring and of which the soul sees only a "dark and doubtful presentiment." With even more certainty than he, we could affirm that the "something" is more than lovers' intercourse, which today is quite readily available without entailing legal or lasting bonds. His use of the word, presentiment, suggests something perceived beforehand, but what? How is it that so many persons who declare they have never known any marriage to be happy, yet retain an expectant hope that for them, under the "right circumstances," it would be so?

It is the thesis of this book that the source of the myth lies in the fact that each human being has indeed had an experience of blissful fusion with another. Every infant begins life in a sort of dream state in which he experiences an illusion of oneness with the mother, not yet able or needing to distinguish "me" from "not me." He does indeed feel "mighty and strong" when his slightest complaint is immediately gratified. Unaware of any separate needs and wishes in the other, he suffers no conflict between self interests and those of persons apart from him. Freud saw this state as one of "primary narcissism," while a later analyst, Michael Balint, described it as one of "primary love." We would instead prefer to call it a state of "primary illusion," for there is as yet only an evanescent sense either of self or of other, only a kind of "harmonious mixup," as Balint termed it.

Inevitably each child must awaken from that dream, and he awakens to a potential dissonance between self and other. He experiences discomforts which are not at once relieved, for the best of mothers cannot always know exactly what her infant wants. He becomes aware that he is not only not omnipotent but even abjectly dependent upon outside succor. Furthermore he finds that mother is not always ready or willing to come to him, that she has preoccupations of her own. So the infant becomes aware, painfully, of himself as separate and his mother as separate, outside and apart from him.

His first attempt to restore that lost paradise is by identifying with the strong parent, creating his self image along the lines of that model, reuniting, so to speak, with his "other half." By imagining himself one with her, he diminishes the felt psychological separation and he partakes of her powers, "mothering himself."

There will be limits to this solution, for, as his motor skills develop, he finds new interests and activities which can be used either to take him away from her or to return to her. Sometimes, however, he finds that he displeases her; he "goes too far," transgresses rules, even gets punished. He learns to curb and channel his activities so that he can preserve the relationship, but he tries simultaneously not to sacrifice his increasingly valued sense of self. Most successful to this end are those pursuits in which he and mother, or father, feel that shared pleasure which serves to augment individual pleasure. Thus is identification restored and reinforced on new levels.

Still there will be areas of conflict between what the child wants or does not want and what the parent wants or does not want. Once more the delicate balance between autonomy and relating can be upset. Now, as speech develops, he uses this new tool to adjudicate the differences, to ask for what he needs and wants, to tell how he feels, and to comprehend the other's needs and wants and feelings. Communication becomes a way to apprehend and avoid serious differences with important others, to enhance the sense of mutual participation through sharing of reactions and to arrive at advanced levels of identification with loved ones.

Throughout life there are three essentials for human fulfillment. The first is for a secure source of "supplies," material and emotional. When the price of these is too high, entailing sacrifice of valued aspects of self, one must be ready to turn to inner sources for a time. The second is for opportunity to exercise one's capabilities, mental and physical, in pleasurable functioning. This requires a context of safety, that is, in which one's own activities and interests do not clash with those of important others, and preferably in which they are appreciated, even mutually enjoyed. The third is for exchange of both thoughts and feelings in such a way that self is asserted and validated and important relationships established and strengthened.

The unceasing search for new and increasingly complex versions of the primary illusion powers much of human development. It can be illuminated by emotional awareness of these essentials for one's self and others, and of the obstacles to their attainment, within and without. For the adult to risk that type of benign regression which love entails he must have achieved a high and relatively secure level of self expansion. Then, as Otto Fenichel described it (1945), "an archaic type of self regard (or even omnipotence) comes back again in an oceanic feeling of losing one's own boundaries."

Jean Sanville

Chapter I

Loving Evolving

More than a century ago, Darwin foresaw an expansion of "man's social instincts and sympathies, with increasing regard for, not only the welfare but the happiness of all his fellow men." He predicted that feelings would become "more tender and widely diffused, extending to all men of all races, to the imbecile, maimed, and other useless members of society, and finally to the lower animals . . ." (*Descent of Man,* 1871).

Elaine Morgan, in *The Descent of Woman* (1972) offers a richly provocative extension of Darwin's work. She advances his view about the evolution of human intimacy: "The whole relationship between men and women should by now be irradiated with a cordial new atmosphere of warmth and comradeship and mutual esteem." She recognizes, however, many sociological difficulties delaying this development.

Between Darwin and Morgan, there has been the slow emergence, then the flourishing of women's liberation which we see as prerequisite for greater equality and empathy between the sexes. Both traditional biology and traditional culture are being transcended (Sanville and Shor, 1973). Despite their conscious and unconscious protests and anxieties, males are, from their deepest motivations, allowing, promoting and favoring the ascent of females, en route to a richer mutuality. Yet men are caught up in an array of obstacles to a fuller empathy with women. The central concern here is with the clinical manifestations and social consequences of some of these difficulties and with the processes of clients as they struggle with these problems.

The psychoanalytic approach makes certain assumptions which are rooted in those basic perspectives which unite biological evolution with psychological development. In his much neglected work on *The Expression of the Emotions in Man and Animals* (1872), Darwin recommends certain principles for "recovering elasticity of mind," principles and methods which anticipate many techniques of several of the very recent humanistic schools of psychotherapy (*Emotional Flooding,* Edit., Olsen, P., 1975). However, these "new" techniques have abandoned the cardinal psychoanalytic discovery: the liberating effect of careful and consistent analysis of transference within the relationship of patient to therapist (Sanville and Shor, 1975). We will illustrate through clinical vignettes the therapeutic values of transference analysis. However, since case examples are always limited and selective expressions of human interaction, and since our disguising of personal identities may distort significant variables, it is necessary to set forth our basic theoretical and clinical approach together with its ethical assumptions.

From Darwin to Psychoanalysis

Because Freud credits Darwin's work as so major an influence in the choice of his own life-work (Kris, 1954) it may be useful to explore the potential relationship between their two approaches to man and mankind (Shor, 1962 and 1963a). Both Darwin and Freud brought a dialectical, developmental principle to bear upon the human dilemma of body-mind (affect-idea) interactions. One established an evolutionary perspective which the other fashioned into a method for further self-conscious evolving. Both social evolution and psychotherapy continue to equip and provoke man to search for greater mastery over and pleasure in his natural resources, within and outside himself. The progress occurs through increasing the awareness, the effective knowing, of the ways and waywardnesses of spirit and energy, of thought and feeling, within oneself and others.

Darwin gathered the data for the theorem that organisms

are capable of change, of growth, of improvement through the development of their structures and functions. Each unit of life has the capacity to develop. The fulfillment of this capacity and its direction of change will depend upon both external and internal conditions. The environmental forces work toward a selective stimulation of organs and functions, constituting body and mind, and result in the natural selection of individuals and species. The internal conditions include not yet definable inherited instinctual potentialities and physical-chemical field conditions which foster or limit these latent possibilities. The individual differences and the processes of heredity are still not well understood. For Darwin, the instinctual forces in this struggle for existence are open to evolution, especially for man (1871). Freud made a detailed study of the open-ended phases of the human drive, from a given biological "impetus" to the variable psycho-social experiences of "source," "aim" and "object" (1905). He too clearly recognizes the inevitablity of cultural forces as causes as well as effects of individual's developments.

Freud absorbed Darwin's developmental approach. He too saw progress as possible, but not inevitable. He also found no evidence for a final design, purpose, or limit to human evolution. He agreed with Darwin that the past lives on in the present, that ontogeny tends to recapitulate phylogeny. And both Freud and Darwin looked to the functioning of the nervous system as the wellspring of psychological experience.

In fact, Freud had been continually at work on these issues in his student days in neurology and neuroanatomy, his experiments with drugs, his studies on aphasia. His special relation to W. Fliess (1892-1903) involved a continuation of his concern with the ideas of evolution and the mind-body dilemma (Kris, 1954). His clinical practice with hysterical patients first included the use of many mechanical and electrical methods that were current in the therapies and theories of that era. Dissatisfied with these, he ventured into the slightly suspect French schools of hypnosis, although insisting that the neural conditions, or character, of the person will limit and influence his suggestibility. Freud reported in many letters his personal dislike of imposing his "will" on the subject, even for well-intentioned therapeutic purposes.

Psychoanalysis begins with the relinquishing of the traditional spirit of benign, authoritarian manipulation. It advances the ethic of respect for self-pacing and self-determination by the patient. The therapist works with a person seeking to measure and regulate its own growth and balance in the use of its energies and resources. This ethical position is part of the humanistic spirit, of course; yet Freud introduced a unique instrument for restoring to the person those aspects of his self-management which were given up to authority figures who seemed to promise help, safety and solutions for inner discomforts.

Freud discovered the workings of transference projections and the principles of interpreting these projections in the immediate, "here and now" context of the psychoanalytic session. Thus he allowed the patient to see and feel his hidden expectations and phantasies both of unrealistic catastrophes and of magical reliefs. When transference interpretations are given gently and correctly, the patient can reconstruct missing links between his experiences of intimacy and autonomy. He spontaneously recalls his past pains and unmet needs, often with a moving reliving of the early editions of these difficult trauma. The respectful, and non-colluding manners of the analyst free the patient to repossess the rights and powers which he had given up and assigned to others. The ameliorative quality of these processes stems from the care with which the clinician helps the patient to recognize, in detail, his particular dreads and hopes, malignant phantasies and benign illusions, while the therapist carefully avoids instructing, advising, prohibiting, judging or punishing. For this loving attention, the professional must also be equipped with an evolving theoretical perspective about human development and interaction as a basis for clear perception of the projections and for offering tentative hypotheses to explain and relieve their workings (Sanville and Shor, 1975).

Beyond Freud some clinicians have deepened the possibilities of transference analysis through new hypotheses and ways of understanding and meeting the earlier, the pre-oedipal and pre-verbal phases of the person's struggle to repair failures and faults in primary relationships, with sources and protectors. Darwin's principles of emotional expression (1972) make much use of the non-verbal experience which dominates these earlier phases of human development (Shor, 1962, 1963a, 1963). Freud came late to consider these primary stages, and his own clinical work tended to avoid the pre-verbal qualities of "instinct" and trauma. He did recognize the difficulties in reading non-verbal expressions and that "silent partner in the psyche," Thanatos (1923), but he was busy refining analytic method and illuminating his classical oedipal theories (Bergler, 1949). However, he did speculate about the crucial role of identification processes in the infant's attempts to master its helpless position. And he stressed the power of phantasy-wishes in fostering illusionary images, like dreaming, to sustain and enrich survival, despite the child's inability to verify and control reality forces. As early as 1898, he wrote that adult happiness derives from "the fulfillment of a childhood wish" (Kris, 1954).

Beyond Freud's Beginnings

Later psychoanalysts have been working toward some further understanding of the complexities inherent in facing uncertainty and ambiguity in infancy and in adulthood. In the absence of firm and manageable reality, urgent drives foster frantic responses. We need to develop "the courage not to comprehend" (Reik, 1937) and a flexibly experimental testing of reality (Shor, 1972). These exploratory states signify a suspension of urgencies and permit a freer examination of alternative solutions. Such processes are in the nature of play, which is the keynote to illusion. The results may be new insights and creative understanding about oneself and about the external world. Both better selfhood and better relating become possible. Clinical psychoanalysis works with the principle that, hidden within every symptom, defense and complaint, there are unconscious wishes to make certain repairs to imperfect, unsatisfactory qualities in oneself or in one's relationship to a significant other.

Theodor Reik's still classical work, *Surprise and the Psychoanalyst* (1937) explores the inner experience of the clinician as he attends to the mixed messages of the patient seeking and fearing help from the presumed authority on whom he has projected magical and monstrous powers. Reik describes the analyst's efforts to maintain a friendly neutrality, suspending both belief and disbelief, refraining from imposing old, easy answers, and remaining open to the surprise, even the shock, of new data, new thoughts, new hypotheses.

A similar courage to endure uncertainty may be manifested today by those "liberated" men and women who experiment with bold positions and actions despite unpredictable consequences. Such brash spirits sometimes produce disasters, and sometimes make valuable discoveries; the consequences depend not only upon their recognition of the social realities but also upon their awareness of self-belittling expectations of threats and punishments and of self-developing wishes to repair and advance inner functions and outer conditions.

If we see in all illusions a core of specific hopes for fulfillment, we have the task of describing the psycho-social conditions and the clinical processes within which a specific illusion can energize the person and guide toward better individuality and better love relationships. And we are challenged to identify the clinical processes of liberating and utilizing the capacities for playing (Sanville, 1975a and 1976).

A "safe space" (Winnicott, 1971) is necessary for a flexible and yet profound playfulness which does not get stuck in either attitudes of triviality or feelings of compulsion. Creative play always tests emerging impulses and phantasies in a current of anxious excitement (Ferenczi, 1923). There are two qualities of danger: abandonment by others and chaotic disorder within oneself. The first is the felt jeopardy of a catastrophic break with one's protective sources, such as parents and the social group. The second is the terror of a fatal fragmentation, a disastrous dissolution of an inner sense of self. These primary anxieties are seen clinically as experiences of being isolated and attacked. A degree of safety from such dreads is necessary for psychic survival and freedom for playfulness.

Traditional forms of social life have always allowed some leeway for play even in very serious institutions such as the Law, the Military and the Church (Huizinga, 1944). Recent social changes in law and public morality have permitted more people to explore modifications and alternatives to established patterns of interpersonal association, in a spirit of relatively new playfulness. Those who feel unable to suspend control, logical purposes, goal-directedness, "will" or rigid rationality, do not risk the uncertainties of trial and error about "right" and "wrong," true and false, real and unreal (Winnicott, 1971). They also will tend to avoid a psychotherapy which works with free-associations and transference analysis. Milner (1955) compares these analytic processes, serious yet playful, to painting in art:

> The frame marks off the different kind of reality that is within it from that which is outside it; but a temporal-spatial frame also marks off the special kind of reality of a psychoanalytic session. And in psychoanalysis it is the existence of this frame that makes possible the full development of that creative illusion that analysts call the transference.

The new cultural tolerance for social and sexual experimentation permits many to venture into fresh qualities of feeling, being and relating. For two types of persons, however, external permissiveness is not enough. Some suffer inner constrictions which prevent utilizing and enjoying available freedoms; they either remain locked into old character roles or, under stress, fall ill with psychosomatic symptoms. Others rush, in poses of a casual manner, to partake of the changing fads and fancies, though they are propelled by eruptive impulses; in time they come to feel worn and wearied, jaded, disgusted with self. Those of the first type are likely initially to seek traditional, authoritarian medical or psychiatric help; those of the second type turn to quick-sell psychotherapies so prevalent in the encounter movement, the growth centers and other popular self-help systems.

Some individuals of each type do make their way to psychoanalytic therapy, still not feeling free. They present themselves as wary about their relationships, professional as well as personal. They try to stabilize and control the therapeutic process, as they do in their personal relationships; for both have come to be felt to be routine and mechanical, lacking the qualities of genuine intimacy. The professional challenge is to engage them with a fresh feeling of freedom in themselves by our clinical effort to illuminate still hidden feelings and phantasies; a major criterion of our success is an increase, in our sessions, of their flexible playfulness, which is also a precondition for intimate loving, with illusion.

Erich Fromm's widely read work, *The Art of Loving* (1956), supported a popular protest against depersonalized sexuality and manipulative relationships. His book encourages a pursuit of spiritual aspects of that "most powerful striving . . . for interpersonal fusion." He helped to distinguish love based on urgent need from that more realistic relationship between two relatively whole persons. However, his sociological analysis emphasized the incompatibility of "capitalism" with "the principle of love." This pessimism is Fromm's presumptive measure for us all that our society does not provide enough safe space. Moreover his work is missing that concept of illusion which might bridge the gap between the individuality and the fusion which he recognizes as desirable. Fromm offers no specific clinical approach to help patients *interweave* these two strivings. Yet he is well known for his critique of a cynical, debunking style and spirit in some orthodox analytic ways of interpreting only the negative forces behind defensive compromises and adjustments. This positive note in Fromm allows for a more optimistic trust that hidden reparative wishes may emerge and lead to a new fulfillment—when there is enough individually felt safe space.

In the 1960's the humanistic movement flourished with its fresh emphasis on self-directedness. There emerged innovations of the orthodox therapy methods, which had turned rigid and authoritarian. The new approaches sometimes appeared with mixtures of oriental philosophies and disciplines adapted to western materialism and technologies. Inspirational messages hover over the array of new therapeutic slogans and gimmicks for people seeking a better fusion of selfishness and togetherness. All the variations of popular "humanism" have included a strain of benign authoritarianism intending to permit a free exploration of personal measures of gratification.

A case in point is the work of Moreno, from the 1930's on. In his *Sociometry and Psychodrama* he instructs people to make practical decisions and to enact assigned roles which are derived from quick, forced associations to the presenting problems; all this is done with no explicit clarification of the therapist-patient relationship, of the transference complications. Under these circumstances, the deeper impacts and meanings of such imposed behaviors do not become available. Although the intent may be a permissiveness, the effect is weakened by the neglect of the patient's initiative, self-pacing and his private right to regulate his own risking or retreating (Shor, 1939).

Many of the popular psychotherapeutic schools have taken an anti-psychoanalytic stance, assuming that all analytic theory and method had become totally rigid. The innovators failed to grasp the uniquely liberating processes of careful transference analysis, which aims, above all, "to give the patient's ego freedom to *choose* one way or the other" (Freud, 1923).

When classical analysts have followed this principle, they come to observe, with Freud, how mature loving includes a regression to infantile wishes and images. Most influential for us, among the orthodox "Freudians," has been Otto Fenichel, who notes (1945):

> It can be stated that at the height of full genital satisfaction identification comes back on a higher level; a feeling of flowing together, of losing one's individuality, of achieving a desired reunion of the ego with something larger which has been outside the boundaries of ego, is an essential constituent of this satisfaction.

This pregnant perception begins to unfold a line of thinking which was taken up more centrally by less tradition-bound psychoanalysts, especially Erik Erikson and Michael Balint.

We see Erik Erikson's sequence of eight stages of psychosocial development as a dialectical series of oscillations between concern with outside and concern with self (1950). For example, he describes the task of adolescence as the finding of one's self, the making of a firm sense of identity; then one can afford to lose oneself in intimacy in the next phase of the spiral. He suggests these ingredients for the "utopia of genitality":

> 1) Mutuality of orgasm, 2) with a loved partner, 3) of the opposite sex, 4) with whom one is able and willing to share a mutual trust, 5) and with whom one is willing to regulate the cycles of work, procreation, and recreation, 6) so as to secure to the offspring, too, all the stages of a satisfactory development.

He acknowledges great difficulties with his own "concrete way" of describing perfect intimacy and he grants that it is "a process which we really do not understand." Yet he does glimpse the creative self-reparative processes in children's play and he glimpses the "taming" effect of "mutual regulation" for adults in sex. However, he does not develop the special positive role for illusion that can refresh the self and renew hopes and efforts toward a model of perfect intimacy. He speaks negatively of the core illusion which we value as model and impetus for development and repair: "The paradise of early childhood must be abandoned—a fact which man has as yet not learned to accept" (Erikson, 1964).

For us, Michael Balint has most richly advanced the understanding of "the mystical union" of mutual loving, in his works on *Primary Love* (1952) and *Thrills and Regressions* (1959). He proposes the theme that:

> This supreme happiness is to a very large extent an illusion, based on a regression to an infantile stage of reality testing. . . . Healthy people are elastic enough to experience this far-going regression without fear, and with complete confidence that they will be able to emerge from it again. . . . It must be a strong ego that can face this danger with equanimity, proud in the confidence that it will be able to emerge from any danger unscathed or even thrilled and refreshed. (1952)

Thus, moments of illusion, of ideal loving, arise from and contribute to the safe psychic space encompassing the two persons, and they expand the energies and capacities for further open-ended growth of each "self" and for the further evolution of their loving together.

The underlying illusion, experienced by both persons in perfect intimacy, is quite specific:

> Primary love is a relationship in which only one partner may have demands and claims; the other partner (or partners, i.e., the whole world) must have no interests, no wishes, no demands, of his or her own. There is, and must be, a complete harmony, i.e., a complete identity of wishes and satisfactions. (Balint, *Thrills and Regressions*)

And the clinical application of this concept is clear:

> There is no fear inherent in the archaic object-love, only naive confidence and unsuspicious self-abandonment: the more paranoid and depressive anxieties and fears have been removed by analysis, the more clearly the phenomena of the archaic object-love—the new beginning in an adult patient—develop before our eyes. (Balint, *Primary Love and Psychoanalytic Technique*)

There are many analysts who have formulated a theoretical perspective which sounds similar to Balint's. For example, Melanie Klein has written (1957):

> Freud described the infant's bliss in being suckled as the prototype of sexual gratification. In my view these experiences constitute not only the basis for sexual gratification but of all later happiness, and make possible the feeling of unity with another person; such unity means being fully understood, which is essential for every happy love relation or friendship. At best, such an understanding needs no words to express it, which demonstrates its derivation from the earliest closeness with the mother in the preverbal stage.

But Klein aims to discourage any renewal of that magical closeness. She stresses the "constitutional" forces of greed and envy as inherent interferences and disruptions which precede any valuing of the source. Idealizations and repaired images of primary love are interpreted only as defensive and disruptive: "The individual feels that he is controlling and exhausting, and therefore injuring it, whereas in a good relation to the internal and external object, the wish to preserve and spare it predominates." And Klein's clinical approach appears to be an insistent verbalistic exposure of the defensive projections of destructive feelings even in idealizations and reparations. No megalomania, autonomy or privacy is to be accepted or enjoyed, not even a benign silence. Klein seems not to work to liberate primary illusion experiences.

Balint questions whether the patient's reactions to imperfect handling, by therapist and by the original parents, should be interpreted only as defensive projections. He postulates a psychic state prior to and contemporary with Klein's paranoid-schizoid position, that of primary love, in which the emerging sense of separate self does experience perfection. The "happy ME" knows no threat or injury to self or other from feelings of controlling and even destroying the supply (1959). He identifies the primary source as a limitless and harmonizing substance, not as an "object." And, in crucial contrast to Klein, he describes his ways of flexible attention to and of silent presence during the delicate phases of preverbal, unspeakable regressions, when the patient's primitive feelings and defenses make verbal, analytic interpretations useless, even taunting (1968).

Balint seeks to facilitate in all patients a transformation of the malignant projections rooted in each person's particular inner history of disruptions, of basic faults, into benign regressions within the transference. From these moments of "new beginning," fresh efforts can then arise to repair those aspects of one's internal heritage which have obstructed the re-experiencing of the magical quality of primary love. This ideal state contains *both* illusions, absolute fusion and megalomanic self-sufficiency. Thus Balint's approach aims to bridge "object-relations" theory and "narcissistic" ego psychology. His beginnings promise the possibility of constructive moments of benign chaos.

"Safe Space" for "Primary Illusion"

We hypothesize that the adult illusion of perfect love has two oscillating aspects, both rooted in the universal infantile experience of primary love, the memory of moments of effortless harmonious, magical union with its source. Supported by a sufficiently perceptive and responsive mother, the baby "experiences" (Escalona, 1968) a non-urgent, smoothly oscillating flow between two states: one-person complete ("Me" secure in all primary narcissistic supplies) and a two-person relationship ("I-You" in perfect harmony) (Shor, 1972). These oscillations imprint a dialectic model which inspires all subsequent drives for fulfillment and for repair of imperfections, however caused.

The moments of feeling successfully met by one's source yield a safety and a freedom to experience all one's sensations in an "harmonious mix-up" (Balint, 1959). In this primary state, there is a global awareness of the mingling of elementary bodily and psychic processes flowing effortlessly between an evanescent sense of "a self" and of "another," easily fusing, incorporating and separating. Thus this illusion contains the quintessence of the "here and now" attitude and also of the spirit of "let it all hang out." It feels like a benign chaos. In contrast, an urgent, unmet drive can provoke desperate activity and force phantasy projections, but this state produces transference cues which, with sensitive interpretation, can lead to a less urgent review of one's inner drivenness.

Real action occurs in moments of illusion too, but there is little felt delay of gratification, mostly the momentary, yet timeless, consciousness of an impulse meeting satisfaction and of energy radiating and discharging into an expanding self and an infinite other. For adults, this primary experience is enriched with the qualities of awareness of self and of relating which were gained in each of the intermediate stages of ego and social development; this multi-dimensional texture characterizes the mutual orgasm between mature adults (Shor, 1954).

Occasions of failure of the primary model are also universal but the types and degrees of imperfection of course do vary. Some delays in gratification are inevitable and gather a supply of undischarged tensions or energies which foster the sense of effort; the resulting work produces ego structures which suspend primary love. The particular imperfections experienced become elaborated into "pathological" influences, with the specific defenses and compromises that make up the character traits and symptoms at each subsequent state of development. The psychoanalytic challenge in therapy is to help the patient re-experience the "basic faults," especially in the transference, and then to help reconstruct the wish for the primary illusion by effective analysis of the paranoid and depressive problems. When the original difficulties, the primary imperfections suffered, are raised to the level of conscious complaint, it becomes possible to rearrange one's resources and efforts and one may then reach more moments of re-experiencing the primary illusion.

In our perspective, people are more alike in their images of original bliss than in their problems and pathologies. The primary illusion is part of the heritage of the psychic unity of mankind; it makes possible occasions of felt perfect loving between persons of profoundly differing cultures, characters and biologies. When persons with such discrepancies leap to meet in an illusion of fusion, they more likely and more quickly fall into incomprehensible feelings of distance and difference, antagonism and confusion, if they have failed to prepare themselves.

Renewing and continuing intimacy requires a clear awareness of one's inner vulnerabilities and a comfortable perceptiveness about any qualities of uneasy responsiveness in the other. Private urgencies produce magical phantasies of immediate and absolute fittingness, without sufficient playfulness between the two. More leisurely exploring could help discover ways to significant pleasure and connectedness. This wider concept of "foreplay" suggests the usefulness of an awareness of one's hidden pains and anxieties as a preparation for pacing oneself, from an urgent phantasy of relief to a playful illusion of fulfillment. Instant intimacies can only serve, at best, as exploratory ventures, for which one needs to estimate one's ability to afford the risks one anticipates. Loving may not yet be earned.

We have applied and extended Balint's ideas and his therapeutic methods. Expanding his concept of primary love, we name it *primary illusion* to facilitate our clinical attention to both aspects of the ultimate human dream, the mutuality and the autonomy. Those babies who are totally deprived of such beatific experiences are not likely to survive (Spitz, 1945). With living patients, we assume that "enough" occasions of good fusion have occurred in infancy. We work with our patients to recognize the presence and the power of this oscillating image of a lost bliss. The patient's recognition and acceptance of the unquenchable wish to regain paradise helps him to relinquish those longstanding defensive positions and maneuvers which have obstructed his reaching a fuller experience of such "ideal" loving and being.

Clinical and Social Prospects

When our work succeeds, we see patients gaining a clearer and stronger sense of self and of the processes of self-growing. Deep anxieties from earlier, more vulnerable phases of life are exposed and alleviated. New feelings of equality and moments of mutuality occur in their therapeutic sessions and then more fully in their intimate lives. They become less submissive to one-sided role-playing in love, work and in the community at large. Each advance in this liberating direction equips them for a richer, fuller sharing with others as well as for a greater flexibility about being separate, private, even alone, at times. They can move with more grace and gratitude (Klein, 1957) between relating and separating, making more realistic use of qualities inherent in themselves and others. Such a spiral of dialectic progression toward "healthy ego strength" facilitates more occasions of fuller fusion in their "object-relations." Thus, when therapy permits a self-determined, safe journey to the re-experiencing of the primary illusion, a new beginning can occur toward the refinement of play, work, and love.

This analytic perspective, with its view of growing through oscillations between advance and retreat, has been recognized by other analysts (Freud, 1938, Greenacre, 1971, and others); but Balint has offered a most startling formulation: "Progression for the sake of Regression" (1959). We are seeing such spirals of preparatory progress and benign regress as patients work to extricate themselves from traditional, rigid sex roles. This is especially evident among women clients, our leading ladies.

The thrust of women's liberation is a challenge to the fatalism of the traditional formula, "Anatomy is destiny." The fresh spirit proclaims the right to greater freedom for individual choice by both women and men. Our analytic ethic agrees with this evolutionary principle. And we find significant support in recent neurological researches reported by Bardwick (1974); rich environmental stimulation promotes a proliferation of dendritic pathways at the neural synapses, and substantially more so when the subject can exercise a flexible freedom of choice. Thus biology as well as society can be responsive to a psychological expansion when resources, safe opportunities and free choice, are provided. The new human data associated with today's liberation movements permit us to see evolving, beyond Darwin's survival criteria for sexual selection, an increasingly personal awareness and expression of private, flexible sexual preference. The general trend we find is toward the valuing of a very individualized ideal of intimacy.

Yet the dialectic of evolution continues. Clients tell us about difficulties and dissatisfactions met during their new pursuits. Many report that instant intimacy and impulsiveness begin to feel tiresome, even dangerous. They may yearn for the comforts and reliabilities of a more stabilized relationship, but they are wary of old marriage ways which spell for them an end to personal growth. Also these explorers complain of embarrassing old edginesses in the course of their ventures; they suffer attacks of jealousy, and they feel anxious about protecting their sense of privacy under the pressure for complete openness and honesty. It becomes evident that further conflicts are being unearthed, and that the ongoing pursuit of perfection requires a fuller development of "fair shares and mutual concern" (Balint, E., 1972). These qualities of shared equality are appearing in new attitudes about economic responsibilities, child care and other aspects of marriage and family life.

In the first phases of our therapeutic work together, patients identify new depths of scarcity feelings in themselves, new kinds of obligation pressures, and different forms of role-playing. These awarenesses of deprivation, suppression and frustration rarely send them back to old answers. Rather, they manifest a courage to claim the best of both old and new worlds. We work to ferret out the felt obstacles, inner and outer, to a vaguely apprehended ideal of consonant loving and being, the model of primary illusion.

Chapter II

From Old Symptoms to New Complaints

The availability of new options within and outside marriage and the family has enabled persons of both sexes to tune in more individually to their inner needs, wants and wishes. Not many years ago no one openly questioned the desirability of taking wedding vows and of begetting offspring. And, once married, there were strong forces, inner and outer, making for the preservation of the union. Man and wife stuck together, enduring deprivations, suppressions and frustrations—and often did not permit awareness of these discontents to attain the level of consciousness. Instead they often developed various physical ailments for which their physicians could find no organic causes: headaches, indigestion, breathing difficulties, heart palpitations, sexual dysfunctions, fatigues, fainting spells and other elusive tensions. They were labelled diagnostically: hypochondriacs, hysterics, anxiety neurotics, phobics, compulsives, obsessives, depressives and more.

Still others manifested hostility, irresponsibility, withdrawal, rebelliousness, alcoholism and other addictions; these persons were often considered "borderline" and even "psychotic." Some more sensitive therapists saw "character problems" in those who tried to make a social virtue of their stoicism and resignation about themselves. Since World War II, psychotherapists have increasingly looked behind the facade of adaptiveness and conformity. As cultural attitudes relieve these private sufferers of the pressure to feel virtuous about accepting their discomforts, the old symptoms are replaced by more direct forms of protest.

Psychoanalytic therapists today rarely see persons with classical neurotic symptoms. Instead patients tend to present a variety of diffuse or specific complaints to the effect that they are not getting out of life what they could achieve or what they are hoping. The new complaints may focus on dissatisfactions with the opposite sex, on dissatisfactions with inner self, or sometimes on difficulties in their ways of relating to one another.

These discontents center around one or more of three types or levels of need: source or "supplies," functioning or self-expression, and interrelating or exchanging. Persons of both sexes need in some degree to receive emotional sustenance even as adults. In the past this has been more overtly allowable for women; men were presumed to be relatively free of the need to depend upon others and had to receive their satisfactions surreptitiously. As for functioning, woman's place was in the home, while far more choices were available for her husband. Couples engaged in recreational activities together sometimes, but frequently with only one making the decision and the other stifling self-interest and going along in an obligatory fashion. In their intimate relations, sexual or conversational, they may have aimed at pleasing each other but often settled for much less than mutuality.

Many societal trends, but most especially women's liberation, are resulting in profound changes. Women are not content to be just the feeders and sucklers. In fact, they are so wary about getting caught up in mothering roles that they sometimes decline them altogether. They want to do things outside the home for worldly rewards such as money, status and power, and not simply to do charitable or volunteer work. And they are demanding better relating, sexually and otherwise. Men are responding with some perplexity. Their gentlemenly inclinations have in part enabled their women to reach for new realms of experience; many men recognize the fairness of women's wanting to be more than wives and mothers. But they may come to balk when their own needs for nurturance are unmet or when they must assume certain of the parenting and homemaking responsibilities formerly delegated to the woman.

These shifts in male-female relationship upset old balances, even create temporary chaos, out of which may emerge new, more satisfying patterns. People may use the disorder both for repairing themselves and for improving the equalities of relating. For these tasks, some do seek professional help.

Deprived

From married women a commonly heard complaint is that their husbands have gradually become undemonstrative, unaffectionate. "He is an excellent breadwinner but I am starved emotionally," is the essence of her discontent. She sees her man as using up all his time and energy in his work or profession, having little or nothing left over for her. Curiously, this complaint is heard even from women whose husbands encourage them to go forth into the world, but this is sensed as a message to "get interested in something and get off my back." Sometimes she finds herself so absorbed in extra-mural activities that she slowly relinquishes her drive for physical contact with her husband. When she comes to realize this, she may either renew her pressures on him to change, or may look to some possible sources in other males, or both.

The husbands of these women plead innocent of any intent to deprive their wives and may profess to care for them very much. They see themselves as straining and striving to assure the welfare or the continued upward mobility of their families. They feel virtuous about their long hours and exhausting expenditures of effort, and perceive their wives' demands for more personal attention as excessive. They are uneasy as they read about heart attacks and ulcers in over-ambitious males, but they cannot easily relinquish their goals. They often report satisfactions in their work relationships which contrast sharply with the dissonance at home.

From the never married career woman, we often hear a degree of envy of her married friends, even when she has learned of their intense dissatisfactions. This discontented woman has usually not felt a sense of choice about her employment and she is caught up in an old prejudice—that there is something wrong with her if she is a spinster. Although often functioning fairly well in her work, she derives minimal gratification from it and is constantly seeking a man to complete her being. She may find one who is willing enough to service her sexually or even to live with her, but who declares his unreadiness to marry, his reluctance to father the children she feels herself wanting. She, thinking her independence is the problem, may even go so far as to give up her career to attend to him.

When we are consulted by such a reluctant man, he may declare his manifest material generosity toward his woman as evidenced in his giving her lavish gifts, taking her on expensive vacations, often expressing a willingness to pay for her therapy. His guilt about depriving her emotionally is not altogether unconscious. He somehow cannot love her, and secretly may harbor suspicions that he cannot love anyone. He is fearful of the infantile dependency which he perhaps accurately senses under the facade of his history of competence at work.

Yet, both the bachelor and the married man, when his woman friend or wife commits herself to serious work or to a profession, finds himself inconvenienced and malcontent. The house is not kept spotlessly clean and neat, meals are haphazard, shirts unironed. If there are children, those come to be his responsibility—to chauffeur, to help with lessons, or even to feed. Perhaps worst of all, if he should be ill, there is no one to take care of him. Unconsciously, he may begin to undermine his companion's independent strivings.

Suppressed

As the man begins to grumble about his self-deprivations, his wife or mistress may react with feelings of being suppressed in her strivings. She notes the reproof in his voice as he comments on unmet needs of the children, and she recognizes his identification with them. She is aware of his resenting doing the dishes on the evenings when she must dash off to classes and of his uneasiness when she is late returning home. She tries to squeeze her school or career homework in with her home homework and at times feels depleted by that endeavor. She may, out of guilt, then relinquish some of her outside commitments, or she may pressure her husband for more household help, either his own or paid. One professional woman announced, "What I need is a wife!"

Some women, especially those who have not had the education for a vocation, claim that they get double messages from their men. On the one hand, they feel pressured to work, either to assist with financial burdens, or just to utilize their good minds. On the other hand, they feel treated as inferiors, their men making the decisions, handling all financial matters or telling them what to do and when and how to do it. These double-binding men may also move into the kitchen and, becoming expert cooks themselves, criticize their women's ability even in this traditionally feminine area.

The man who thus push-pulls his woman often finds fault with her that she does not leave him enough time-space to do his thing. He too perceives himself as suppressed. He has become aware of her resentment at his over-time in the office, or at his bringing his work home. When he attempts to lay aside his work worries by reading or watching a ball game on TV, she takes that as an opportunity to interrupt, he complains, "always wanting attention." He has a conscience, however, about her discontents and wishes her to participate at least in his recreational activities, fishing, sailing, skiing, and he feels rebuffed when she responds with disinterest. Sometimes he pursues his own play interests separately, but with an uneasy feeling about what his wife or woman may be doing or feeling meanwhile. Or he may, affirming the value of his separate functioning and pleasures, and sensing the impossibility of significant sharing, try to muster the courage to leave her.

Frustrated

He is most likely to contemplate separation when he has allowed himself rather fully to experience his frustration about the relationship. Often the man chooses this particular woman out of his male-chauvinist needs. He has wanted to feel superior, to play the dominant role, and he has needed a woman upon whom he could project the infantile dependent aspects of himself. The man who enters psychotherapy has often become conscious of the limitations of this kind of arrangement. He has wearied of being the leaning post for his mate. Experiencing dependency mainly vicariously has left him feeling still deprived. He has had enough of guilt about pursuing selfish interests; it has left him feeling suppressed even when acting upon his own pleasures. The compliance of his woman is beginning to be experienced as coming from a sort of nonperson. He wishes to talk with her but finds himself talking down to this relatively uneducated, ignorant mate, whose chatter about house and children or about volunteer activities leaves him bored.

Sex with her has become not significant. He may continue to make love to her in a token fashion, but it is no longer exciting to him. Sometimes his loss of interest renders him virtually impotent with her, or at least renders his performance inadequate—both to himself and to her. To reassure himself he sometimes experiments with other women, but—even when successful sexually—he usually feels an inadequacy about this solution.

The woman, who has often depended for her self-esteem on her obvious attractiveness to her man, feels some jeopardy in his diminishing ardor. If he is still making some effort, she may querulously demand, "Why only on Saturday nights?" Frequently she is suspicious that there must be someone else. If he performs inadequately, she either grows angry in her disappointment or solicitous about his problem, perhaps suggesting sex therapy. She may find herself tempted to have affairs and may succumb to those impulses, generally also reporting initial excitement but short-lived gratification in such a scheme.

Her chief dissatisfaction with her man tends to be that his verbal communication with her is lacking in emotional expressiveness. She describes how he tries to listen but she senses that his thoughts are elsewhere. "He doesn't really hear me," she declares. Or, at best, she does sometimes sense a sort of indulgence in his patient attention to her pouring out of her joys and sadnesses, as though such expressiveness was beneath him. She attempts, in every way that she knows, to get him to reciprocate, to let her know what he is experiencing and feeling. It is, she relates, as though she asked him to speak with her in a foreign tongue, for he may not even know what she means by her request that he express his feelings.

Self-complaints

So long as the complaint is about the "other," the request is likely to be for couple therapy. Or, if the partner is reluctant about professional help, then the seeker, usually the woman, begins to listen to and look at herself more deeply. What she often finds are the inner reflections and echoes of the faults which she once assumed to be outside. She comes to see the inadequacy of her inner supplies, how her precarious self-esteem depends on her man. She feels a terror of her aloneness, for she senses her own emptiness. She may satisfy the inner gnawing by eating, and the ensuing obesity damages still further her self-image. She may drink excessively, and the shame at being out of control or unconscious leaves her feeling more inferior and unworthy.

Many women suffer mild or not-so-mild depression as they consciously or unconsciously sense the extent of their dependency on outside confirmation. "I am depressed although I have everything—a prominent husband, beautiful home, lovely children, opportunities to travel, . . ." may be her opening statement to her therapist.

She feels burdened, bored yet obligated about housework and mothering, and these feelings are unrelieved by her leisure pursuits. She begins to cast about for what else she might do with her life, and is discouraged if she is without work skill. She may attend some consciousness-raising groups which further alert her to her plight, and her women friends in careers may exhort her to seek a vocation of her own. Although she is frightened if she has spent years being "only a housewife," or if she has settled for a mundane job pending a hoped-for marriage, she finds plenty of support and encouragement from the female world of today.

She may start out with feelings of inferiority to her man, but as she overcomes her sense of incompleteness as a person and as she comes to enjoy exercising her own powers and skills, she more often than not arrives at a self-evaluation which is that she is superior. This tends to eventuate if he has been totally resistant to looking into himself, and then it is almost inevitable that she plays with the idea of parting from him.

It may take the imminent threat of being abandoned to catapult the man into treatment, so dangerous to his homeostasis does he perceive the inward look to be. When he musters the courage, he, too, often discovers a felt paucity of inner source, discovers his hidden dependencies upon the woman he viewed as leaning on him. He too experiences depression at his essential aloneness, and also feels empty although he may try to drown out such anguish with his buddies at the bar, or in increased work commitment.

He sometimes can move to an awareness of some envy of his woman's ability to laugh and to play. He permits himself to recognize a certain boredom with his work and notes that it has rendered him a dull boy. Phantasies of alternatives often contain hints of secret wishes to partake of roles once deemed feminine. To help people, for example, often appeals greatly to the man who perceives himself as having been in the business of exploiting others. He comes to consider impulses to do more than just earn money or even to gain prestige. He wishes to accomplish something about which he can feel proud.

Depending upon what his woman has been doing, he may come to feel either inferior or superior to her. But, if the former, he can begin to make attempts to develop in himself the qualities that he admires. He is no longer ready to settle for mere superiority and he moves to promote his mate's further unfolding—or to leave her.

Inadequate Intimacy

The quality of intimacy experienced by each person at any stage of life is a variable composite of three processes or ways of connectedness: communication, participation, and identification. The individual's innate temperament and psycho-social history shape the developmental phases, which vary in the predominance of one mode or another. Thus any moment of feeling closeness has its unique ratio of these three processes, and the experience of what is necessary for perfect or "good-enough" intimacy will vary from person to person and from phase to phase. The therapist is called in to help in periods generally when a client is missing links to a vital other.

The inquietudes described to us by our patients add up to

dissatisfaction with the level of mutuality attained between the sexes. They do not have a sufficiently reciprocal relationship. They do not give and receive equally. Relationships between unequals always harbor certain actual and phantasied exploitations and resentments. Such unequal relating evokes difficulties in identification, in participation and in communication.

Identification

The capacity to identify, to feel as one with the other, is surely the first prerequisite to intimacy. Yet what we observe in unsatisfactory relationships is that each identifies with an aspect of the other, not with the whole person. These identifications with "parts" are tenaciously clung to because the other comes to represent qualities of self that are not yet claimed or owned.

For the male, most especially those brought up to enact the strictly traditional masculine instrumental role, the woman-of-choice has often been she who most precisely embodies the qualities not permitted to him: weakness, dependency, emotionality, frivolity, the whole range of expressiveness. He supports and protects her and attempts thereby a vicarious gratification of his own concealed needs and wishes. If and when he becomes dissatisfied with this arrangement, he is harassed by inner misgivings, for he can imagine her pain should he abandon her. Moreover, he may sense that, if alone, he will be confronted within himself with the very qualities that he has heretofore projected upon her. Thus he stays hooked-in, envying her the protective parenting, the very gift that he gives her, unable either to move away or to wholeheartedly help her to develop toward the relative independence and resourcefulness he thinks he wants in her.

For the traditional female, brought up to see her role in life as that of wife-mother, the identification may be with the work-role of her husband or lover. She wins status and prestige when her man is successful, achieving, respected. Thus, although she may abortively attempt to get him to tone down his ambitions, to give less of himself to his business or profession, there may be a hidden reservation about such ends so long as she has not learned to use her own capabilities in the world away from him.

That identification which leads to constructive empathy is based on the capacity to imagine the whole texture of the other's experience. It permits a momentary dipping in, merging with the self of the other, then a return, so to speak, to one's own psychic skin, with a return to a feeling of private completeness which however now includes the deeper awareness of the other. The degree of willingness to risk such temporary losing or lending of one's self depends on one's estimate as to whether the other's feeling state might enhance or threaten one's own individuality. Such private measures are influenced by hidden phantasies both magical and monstrous. The risks surely include the problems of primitive envy (Klein, 1957). At its best the understanding and compassion expressed may afford a relief and dissipation of pain, sadness and other discomforts; so also may feelings of joy, delight and expansion spread and be shared. Then the act of identification can become both a valued gift and a confirmed sharing.

Participation

It is the inner sense of having the same experience psychologically and even physiologically in joint activities that makes shared active involvement contribute to intimacy and to the enrichment of individual experience. On this basis it can confirm, deepen, and extend the previously imagined identification, and can enhance each individual's separate experiencing. Without such equal and flexible co-experiencing, a submissive dependency develops in which one of the couple goes along with the other but would be fearful of doing the action alone. Thus one young woman patient, shy to the point of terror with people, accompanies her lover to innumerable social gatherings where he proudly shows off her exotic beauty, but she is miserable, knowing he will later chide her that she did not speak. She dreads these occasions but permits herself to be dragged to them in the hope of inuring herself to her anxieties.

Another kind of problem arises when two people like to engage in the same pursuits but their levels of skill are unequal and the activity is of different degree or type of significance to each. One couple recently complained that their skiing weekends were never "together-times," since the husband, an old expert, took to the steep runs, while she, a novice, clung to the bunny-slopes. He did not wish to be responsive to her consequent complaints of aloneness since his pleasure was in the challenge of performing on the difficult inclines.

Thus such discrepancies in abilities can create temporary obstacles to comfortable experiencing of both intimacy and individuality. But when the differences in skill or value are felt as secondary to the drive for increasing closeness and connectedness, then efforts are made to share verbally the separate meanings and feelings. A process of communication evolves with a safe friendly flexibility for individual growth and for sharing experiences; non-verbal cues and signals join in the sharing of feelings toward a sense of joint identity.

Communication

Interchange of thoughts, ideas and feelings is generally understood to be another prerequisite to good relating. But the complications of communication can be many and varied.

The most common complaint is by the woman to the effect that her man does not really talk with her other than about surface matters. Her yearning is for mutual interchange about feelings and the nuances of personal unfoldings. She has often tried to impart to him her own emotions, her reactions to stresses and pleasures, but in the absence of his reciprocating, she may give up her effort.

In an attempt to salvage a sense of connectedness, they may converse about areas of necessarily joint involvement, the house, the children, maybe recreational plans. Stumbling blocks are met even here, for in the discussion about such matters, feelings of discontent arise about inadequate sharings of self on more intimate levels, including the non-verbal aspects of sexual loving.

Thus, a frequent stalemate in dissident pairs is that one partner, usually the woman is reduced to a reiteration of felt needs, while the other is complaining about being talked at and nagged. We also often hear about a wife's enduring in boredom her husband's daily recital of business or work details.

Communication, at its best, involves an effort to relate and explain one's central meanings and values to a reciprocally respected other who will comprehend and appreciate one's essential thoughts and feelings. Each partner will offer this to the other, and both will feel well met. Then a dialectical dialogue can develop, and enhance the feelings of identification and the sense of participation.

A Spiral of Fresh Aspirations

Those who proceed in psychotherapy sense to some degree that they do not yet know enough about their wishes and potentialities to make choices and decisions in life. They have still to recognize and explore private terrors which obstruct making their own next ventures for growth and gratification. They come to feel freer of urgencies to impulsive and compulsive action and can then respond with less desperation about decisions. In these easier states, hopes and wishes, long latent, emerge in the context of the present.

Women more often than men take the initiative in seeking psychotherapy. They come with a wide variety of complaints; many with a vague discontent about life, with feelings of depression or boredom. Other women come with very specific dissatisfactions about their relationships with men. Sooner or later nearly all focus on their lack of fulfillment as individuals. They see the complications of combining the aspirations for self and for loving but they remain determined to find ways to coordinate both of these hopes.

As the woman gains a heightened awareness of her inner life she wishes to share that new richness with husband or lover. There may be an increased frustration when he is not able to respond in kind, to share with her *his* inner processes—or perhaps not even able to comprehend her. This may then lead to her urging him to enter therapy too. More often than not, he will be reluctant to do so.

The men respond with a variety of defenses. The more traditional males may allow their wives to continue in therapy, with the hope that "the doctor" will cure the wife of her "silliness," and get her to stop haranguing him. Or, if he is overly rigid, and feels threatened by his wife's expansiveness, he may refuse to pay for further therapy. The braver men may allow themselves to be led to the therapist's office, however reluctantly, and permit themselves to feel degrees of discomfort, as they listen patiently and perhaps with interest. Some may find a cautious way to continue some participation; for example, he may suggest that he will be available for another appointment whenever the therapist thinks he can be of help, as though to serve as co-therapist. Some will agree to a series of conjoint sessions. The most courageous may soon arrange for their own individual psychotherapeutic search as they have permitted their women to do. These are the gentle men who glimpse richer possibilities in a more open sharing of feelings and aspirations (Sanville and Shor, 1973).

The clinical impression that it is the ladies who lead has been reinforced by colleagues who work with persons from lower socio-economic strata where men are even more bound to "instrumental" roles (T. Parsons, 1951). Women want liberation for men as well as for themselves; they recognize the inevitable interdependence. Sociological speculation will suggest that since women are generally closer to the intimately expressive and dependent functions, they will have the skills and know the satisfactions in such experiences. Their reliance on men as the sources of protection and basic supplies in living encourages them to lend their empathy to their dependable mates. Thus women are reaching for both worlds, the expressive and the instrumental, and they aspire to intimate relationships between two newly equal partners.

These clinical data and sociological impressions have made necessary a reconsideration of the traditional analytic hypotheses about male-female development and about our methods of professional help. We approach both of these issues, as they bear on the main theme of this book, in the next four chapters; more general and more technical examinations of basic theory and method are attempted in the two appendices.

Chapter III

Approaching the New Patient

It was a woman who initiated the clinical method of psychoanalytic therapy. In presenting his very first case, in 1895, that of Frau Emmy Von N., Freud admits that his well-meaning "prohibitions and instructions . . . had been ineffective." Following this, he reports: "She then said in a definitely grumbling tone that I was not to keep on asking her where this and that came from, but to let her tell me what she had to say." His reaction was not defensive: "I fell in with this, and she went on without preface. . . ." Within a few years of further clinical work with such spirited women he developed the principles of free-association and the interpretation of unconscious conflicts. The psychoanalytic method was well begun.

Current Complaints about Psychotherapies

Women are still protesting that many psychotherapists even today instruct and prohibit, both overtly and covertly. Their antagonism to the old psychoanalytic view of females has led many to venture into other therapies which promise quick and sure cures to problems previously thought to require years of couch and consultation. Each season yields such a crop of innovative methods that searching patients have an ever-widening choice. Tiring of dutifully following directives, or leery of libertarian enticements, or overwhelmed with spates of inspirational messages, or insulted by shallow and sloganistic atmospheres, or suspicious of personal prejudices or power-seeking behind the seeming spirit of benign patriarchal guidance, some individualistic persons sometimes retreat to their own, less professionalized pathways for consciousness-raising and self liberation.

Initial enthusiasms for each of these ways are often followed by disappointments that usable insights are not gained, either for significant personal change or for the attainment of more profound relating. Now we see a tentative returning to psychoanalysis in the hope of receiving more sensitive attention to individual complaints, conflicts, hopes and fantasies. But this time, patients demand that archaic notions be dropped, that traditional presumptions be put aside, that they be helped to discover their own next needs and ultimate wishes and that they be equipped to make their own measures and choices at their own private pace. Even those pleased with their previous psychoanalytic therapy may start again but now with a wish to reduce the self-observing and the self-analyzing they do and to work through to more spontaneity, fun and courage to risk new ways. They want more playfulness in life.

Perhaps most of us, as therapists, have experienced conservative clinical moments when we favor a patient's return to a "safe" marriage or work situation because we feel that person's "ego" is too "weak" or that the social or economic realities should discourage new ventures; we have been trained to make diagnostic formulations and to "define the basic problem." Ethical humanists today are unlikely to make explicit prohibitions or admonitions, but patients are sensitive to our hidden prejudices, and may dare to report that even well-meaning biases feel like pressures and invasions. They resent others' taking the measures of their pains and pleasures. When the clinicians succeed in recognizing their own impositions or temptations to guide, they can avoid violating patients' self-measure. Free of that burden and responsibility, therapists can better attend to the spontaneous wishes for self-repair in the patients' phantasies and projections as expressed in their treatment.

When a therapist entertains libertarian impulses for patients, there is danger of engendering an opposite effect, that of provoking more impulsiveness and risking than is manageable. Such open biases are more easily identifiable by the patient. These "progressive" pressures also fail to promote that deeper self-awareness and choice which we believe can be our major contribution (Shor, 1977).

The ethic of self-determination finds its greatest challenge from those who, facing new dilemmas of decision, criticize us for insufficient feedback to their stalemates (Shor, 1961). They complain that they cannot make a choice and even ask us directly to advise, to offer a measure. In a spirit of friendly neutrality, we can identify to them the urgency, or even desperation, to force a decision and to avoid the specific anxieties about their not yet knowing or understanding enough. Those who feel they cannot tolerate such ambiguity may leave us and seek more directive helpers, in which our society abounds. In our clinical experience, it is mostly males, even the gentle men, who request precise answers in the mode of their traditional, instrumental role-functioning.

The new complaints presented to the psychotherapist contain a fresh thrust toward individualistic self-concern which defies established limits. These nascent noises of dissatisfaction and demand break through the sound barriers even in the sound-proof offices of professional helpers. More and more men and women are resisting and rejecting classical psychiatry and psychoanalysis. There is indeed a necessity now to rethink traditional concepts and to revitalize psychoanalytic method. We will describe our modifications in working with these pioneering patients.

Facing Females at the Mäch

Women are particularly wary of presenting their personal confusions and restless discontents to male doctors. This is especially so for women who have had a traditional patriarchal father. The male professional will be put to tests, both deliberate and unconscious. If the patient begins in early consultations with a direct questioning of the therapist's viewpoints, the response must include a direct reply. Though we expect that her doubts will run deeper and return in subtler, hidden ways, it is important to respect the strength of her first forthright challenges by a simple statement of the intent to be non-judgmental. A sophisticated consultee may suggest that professional training and personal biases will complicate the aim to remain neutral. That possibility is granted but she is invited to alert us to what appear to be infractions, slips or manipulations. If an atmosphere of a cooperative venture is achieved, the patient proceeds to describe her particular dilemma.

The female patient approaching the female therapist is more likely to assume she has an ally here. In fact, she often reports previous consultation with a male therapist whom she saw to be judgmental about some of her new ventures and to be relegating her to her "proper" role as wife-mother. However, she may later discover that she has harbored, on a less conscious level, apprehensions that, after all, her female therapist may turn out to be a moralistic mother. Thus women therapists too may be suspected of fostering a "realistic" adaptation by resignation and manipulation, not permitting self-discovery and exploration beyond traditional role-playing. The alert therapist will expect to be tested for the presence of hidden attitudes and will enable the patient to identify such transference projections.

From the initial sessions with male or female therapist, patients come to identify themselves in three broad ways: 1) as fighting rebels who are protesting the oppressiveness of husband, law, morality and such "establishment" forces; they are mostly angry but wish to learn to be equipped emotionally to do battle, 2) as fleeing outcasts who wish to run away from an unsatisfying life style, but feel guilt and fear about abandoning the safe nests or the young children; they suffer oppression by their own consciences and yet daydream of plots to evade facing the authorities, the internal and the external threats, 3) as defeated downcasts who feel helpless and depressed; they can hardly express protest or fancy flights but wait for us to discover in them the energy to find some solution. These attitudes may occur at various times in one person.

However the dilemma is presented, each patient reveals a pattern of conflicted phantasy—on the one hand, of being caught in an unbearable situation, and, on the other, of feeling driven toward drastic action. Neither solution feels acceptable. It is for the patient herself to choose whether she wishes to make compromises and adjustments. It is so frequently evident that patients are relieved and feel encouraged when we give back their freedom and responsibility to make their own decisions or to suspend plans and actions while they continue to explore confusions and stalemates, within themselves, in their homes, work, and society at large.

They then come to use their sessions in earnest experimentation with imagined glimpses of alternative ways of relating to the feelings and forces confounding them. They experience cycles of challenging us, feeling relieved and regaining their freedom to speak from within with safety; these spirals work to foster a sense of flexibility about the therapist, and then about themselves. They increase their free associating and an attitude of "play" begins to emerge in the "safe space" (Winnicott, 1971).

A child playing in its crib, play-pen, sandbox or park, relies on more than safety. It expects confirmations and corrections for its assertions and expressions. It welcomes and enjoys these processes which relate its spontaneous thrusting to a recognition and validation, explicit and implicit, from the powers who are also his protectors and suppliers. The child's attention oscillates from self to the other, ideally at a spontaneous pace which produces a minimum of oppression, suppression or depression. Such sensitive responsiveness is the most delicate task for the "good-enough" parent, and for the "good-enough" therapist.

To ready ourselves for these subtle nuances in our patients' attitudes, we must continuously attend to our inner comfort. For this, professional training requires personal therapy which, ideally, equips us to continue self-analytic awareness. Our ongoing inner search promotes the maturing of our private positions and processes. This personal responsibility is intrinsic and crucial to our professional task, yet it is the most subjective, the most difficult aspect of the therapist's preparation. All training institutes contend with the complexities of effecting and estimating the emotional readiness of the trainee-therapist.

While these uncertainties persist, a patient's complaints about the therapist cannot be treated only as resistances and projections. We must take in their criticisms and watch for hints of unverbalized doubts about us. We must be able, internally, to scan and sift through the tones of the patient's discomfort for resonances with ourselves.

When familiar themes in a patient's self-complaints echo experiences of our own, we privately review the processes toward resolution which we discovered. Too quick an assumption of similarity may be a leap over subtle but significant differences. Cautious use of empathy helps us to see the patient's stalemate in its own uniqueness, but drawing on the psychic unity of humankind, enables us to develop tentative hunches about the missing elements in his or her awareness of self. Forging hypotheses from both the general and the particular, we offer interpretations which may assist the patient to turn an angry, anxious or depressive rut into a fertile furrow for future growth.

Today's unfamiliar complaints alert us to be even more hesitant and tentative about interpreting the problem. The clinical danger here is that the therapist, eager to be "helpful," may impose an abstract theory or worse, a moral or ethical assumption of his own. Women patients have frequently reported that previous therapists have failed them in both ways: "head trips" and "old-fashioned," "conventional," "clichés," or "practical" suggestions and encouragements.

How can the clinician prepare to hear the unfamiliar, the new feelings and phantasies from foraying females? The therapist must first know and confirm to himself his own quiet comfortable center. Then he can take this easy sense for granted and make space for the venture of a journey following the new complaints and hopes of his patients.

In this direction we have valued Theodor Reik's *Surprise and the Psychoanalyst* and other descriptions of the inner experience of non-intrusive, open-minded and open-hearted listening and silent presence. Members of the "Middle Group" in the British Psychoanalytic Society (M. Milner, 1955, 1969; W. Winnicott, 1965, 1971; M. Balint, 1932, 1952, 1959, 1968; and perhaps, W. Bion, 1970) have also pioneered this subjective area of psychotherapy, more than have the disciplined members of the proper Freudian or the brash Kleinian schools of therapy, as we see it. These less doctrinaire people have been finding a place for play and for illusion in the texture of the human condition in evolution. They have enriched Freud's classical principle of transference analysis to allow for change, discovery and creativity beyond the established limits and standards. They have prepared us to listen, with a third ear as well, to the confused gropings of patients, especially today's women, evolving beyond the known.

Both silences and interventions are intrinsic to effective communication. A good silence in the therapist bespeaks a trust that the client can adventure safety and usefully into her own dark places. The therapist meets her angry, anxious messages with low-key, tentative interpretations which may give her insights into her own lack of confidence to make the venture. When we have accurately mirrored her inner state, a pause, a moment of quiet, occurs between us; a new friendly space is felt in the immediate present. The sense of relief is visible in the softened look and posture of the patient. Freer associations will then flow. And her easier mind and voice begin to poke softly inside, closer than any outsider, even the most intuitive therapist, can ever touch.

When the patient presents the new products of her probing and inner sensing, we feel invited to recognize and receive these new data as her provisional discoveries. We are engaged to follow and match the sensitivity and flexibility of the patient. We must learn to listen so that we can hear a further invitation before we offer our tentative hypotheses about possible links between the old, known and the new, unknown wishes and fears. The working alliance proceeds with these emerging products of exploratory play. Discovery and intuition do not thrive in an atmosphere of formality and ritual. Yet there must be a sense of safety from intrusions and invasions which pressure the patient's central search for clarity about her inner self. In our practice no rigid schedule or frequency of sessions is imposed, although, of course, our practicalities and convenience frankly set limits to the patient's requests.

Yet the working alliance for therapeutic cooperation is here recognized, at times even explicitly, as a partnership which is not one of simple equality in all significant aspects. Some head- heart- and foot-loose therapists favor sharing their own "hang-ups" with the patient and they muddle in with "equal" existential pronouncements about life's dilemmas. Such sharings are widely, even inescapably available anyway from family, friends and philosophers. Although the therapist who owns his quiet center may derive his observations and interpretations in part from private processes of growth and awareness, he does not impose his particulars on the patient. Personal exchanges divert the client from his own unique strains and resources. Our special professional contribution is to provide a non-intrusive context for his or her maximal self-exploration. The patient's inner disquiet may stir him to seek confidences from the therapist instead of examining his self-doubts, his own lack of confidences.

When do we intervene? How do we formulate and express our hints and hypotheses? If we were primarily intent on exposing the defensive, evasive aspect of the patient's symptoms and complaints, the patient might, in her distress, be impressed with our manner of superior certainty. Our clever message might work to persuade her to submit to our secret ways and wisdoms. "Transference cures" occur; some may even endure, as enthusiastic testimonials often proclaim. But the person hiring the therapist has been discouraged about her own powers and deprived of the pleasures in reaching and discovering her own possibilities, because of the correctional atmosphere, with its subtle tones of condescension, disapproval and debunking. The spirit and the manner of our interventions and silences are crucial considerations; each successful occasion affords the patient the illusion of effortless, safe autonomy, and she can internalize this model as part of her own equipment for life after the therapy has terminated.

If our intent to respect the patient's readiness to invite our intervention is communicated, we are often forgiven for the errors we make in premature or imprecise comments. From these transgressions, we may learn the particular pace and pathways of the specific person we are attending. The permeating ethical principle we are propounding for the therapeutic relationship, so simply illustrated in Freud's response to Emmy Von N., is a pervading clinical guide for work with the subjectivities of self-liberating women thrusting and thrashing into unclear realms.

The bold ones exercise and experiment with new arrangements of personal and social relationships, and they produce the discoveries and the disasters which provoke, forewarn, inform and tease the rest of us. These adventurers explore outside the tenets of established morality. Many of us feel liberal enough to call for greater community tolerance toward trial and error; we suspend firm, old distinctions between the brave and the foolish. The deprecating clichés about females are disappearing and more safe space for creative play is being provided. But when anyone feels threatened beyond his private estimates of emotional safety, defensive measures are instituted. Thus even scientists and therapists may balk, block, belabor and bedazzle their charges (Shor, 1970). Most of our society is confused by the new sounds and flurries of women at the mäch.

As new freedoms of choice emerge, some women show an early phase of petulant demanding for themselves those prerogatives which men have monopolized: money, status, power. Most of our patients move beyond this, aspiring to a richer sharing with their mates of the practical and emotional gratifications and burdens of old roles, male and female.

Meeting Males in Accommodation and Retreat

The clinical evidence for masculine reticence in this era of feminine forwardness must be seen in historical perspective. We owe an appreciative word for the tradition of male chauvinism. Many frontiers have been expanded by heroic men: geographical explorers, profit-seeking pioneers in commercial exploitation, robber barons, populist revolutionaries, daring and spirited scientists. Yet many of these benefactors were frankly sexist, and racist, in behavior and attitude. Although these powerful men have traditionally put down women as second-class, immature and inferior, though very useful, males did produce technologies, material supplies, social safeties, legal principles, scientific concepts and methods which have and are facilitating the progress of women to equal participation in political, economic and social realms previously simply ruled out. Men at large have supported their women in their basic needs, and some have begun to foster female efforts to develop to their own fuller humanity.

At least equally significant for the further evolution of human relationships is that the dominating male functioned as conservator of human sensitivity; he did lovingly protect the subordinate female, providing both supplies and safe space that she might develop, for us all, the capacities for expressiveness and playfulness, for dreams and illusions. In these realms, he frequently accepted a second-class, inferior status. His pride and pleasure in her accomplishments signify more identification than actual participation or communication; therefore his possessiveness remained relatively infantile and was permeated with an undercurrent of destructive envy and of anxiousness about losing a valued source. Here is a keynote to our clinical problem with men in this area of women's liberation, when both sexes face profound and unpredictable developments. The dependent yet expressive role of women has equipped them to feel freer to use a psychotherapeutic approach which consciously and deliberately favors playfulness and illusion in the service of more flexible efforts and decision-making. Men are less prepared. They are suspending much of their chauvinist posturing and impositions, but they are only slowly permitting themselves to be prodded by their women into that fuller, subjective humanity which men have so valued, if secretly, in their mates.

Married men, however, are uneasy about our clinical approach. They are less willing, so far, to carry their therapy through all the cues we glimpse. Those feeling their inferiority most acutely announce a revengeful demand that the two sexes first divide the old burdens and miseries. A few men in fact become so antagonistic to mate and therapist that they withdraw financial support and make ultimata about conformity to traditional roles. Their women counter by fighting even more desperately. These battling relationships, as we see them in our work, rarely survive. The gentler male mates do make appearances in our offices, showing much shock and confusion. They allow leeway for their ladies: for continued therapy, for further education and for exploring work possibilities, preferably part-time. These tolerances, seen in treatment process, contain compromises, made by the husbands, between their need to keep control and their wish to help mates reach for richer lives and perhaps to become more equal partners. Married males generally remain caught in old, emotional rigidities until they feel that their venturing females are threatening to leave, or even to defy a particular advantage or control which the male holds most dearly.

Thus one husband, long resigned to domestic impotence

and the occasional sexual escapade, discarded his wife when she declared directly her right to foreign affairs. Yet this disruption of his long-standing arrangement led to several months of anxious confusion which brought him to seek therapy. He soon recognized his admiration and envy for the straightforwardness which his wife had displayed. He also reviewed his secret pleasure in the fun projects and travels which she proposed during the years of their compromise arrangement. Her limited playfulness had been indulged with condescension on his part. His fear of "whole-hearted fun" was both cause and effect of his traditionally split life. We worked to locate and alleviate the hidden sources of this fear. Meanwhile, he has come to agree to a less vindictive settlement with his former wife, and he is proceeding with the serious therapeutic tasks within himself. He is determined to liberate his own sense of open play rather than return to old positions.

The inner obstacles to abandoning archaic "advantages" loom especially large in men mated to weak, immature women. The search for a new, repaired self requires accepting a humble posture not easy for the established hero who has many alternative social outlets. Thus, as women succeed in revising further the public atmosphere, more men may accept professional help for their struggles with the consequences of the new cultural climate. Meanwhile, for married men, our clinical observations are less intensive. We may be experiencing an era of distinctly more distaff data in our work; perhaps this is so since women have been more dependent and exploited and are now actively complaining and searching. Further female freedom may necessarily precede our fuller clinical study of male inner life.

Unmarried men are more frequently willing to be patients. They have already chosen not to use available conventionalized supports and screens for their needs and imperfections. They may be readier for the voluntary self-exposure which psychotherapy signifies. We are here considering the functioning person who is not displaying that severe pathology which pressures community or family measures of self-defense. He is choosing to seek a more self-determined, spontaneous and creative individual fulfillment.

Our unmarried male patients today are pursuing new ways

of attaining richer intimacy without loss of valued autonomy. They do not aspire to old patterns of marriage relationship. They too grope for some new forms of flexible mutuality and, like female patients, do not seek advice or authority for a "best" model of fulfillment. They call on a therapist for help in removing inner fixations and confusions which block their individual search for more perfect loving.

If our professional colleagues will confirm these clinical impressions about attitudes to psychotherapy on the part of married and unmarried males, we feel encouraged to interpret the relative reticence of married men toward therapy as support for the speculation that the act of marriage has traditionally contained, hidden within its culturally protected confines, a core illusion of eventual perfection through identification and possessiveness alone. As urgency about survival decreases, the wishes for more participation and communication emerge and expand. The increasing frequency with which divorce occurs suggests that the narrower, concealed illusion rooted in identification alone is being discarded; this may permit a more conscious and deliberate pursuit of a new edition of loving. This is our clinical perspective and a principal guide to the unconscious meanings within the complaints of patients, male and female. Our thesis of an original, inevitable and undying wish for a perfect primary love can thus be seen as the rationale for helping each patient become aware of the hidden expression of that hope, behind the pains and poses in his current life.

Confronting Couples

That males are more "defended" against that hope is evident in their reluctance either to acknowledge complaints, or to follow their wives into therapy. Quite regularly it happens that when the wife has, in treatment, experienced intensely her own wishes and capacities for fuller mutuality, she attempts to persuade her husband also to seek professional help, for she views his character as an obstacle to her fulfillment. Although threatened by his spouse's newly aroused strivings toward independence, he is likely to resist any suggestion that he needs help. If their relationship permits, she may, by emulating the spirit and style of her therapist, enable him to acknowledge his fears about self-exploration. Sometimes these feel to him insurmountable, but he may be able to accept some exploratory sessions when he can see them as "for the sake of the children" or "for our relationship," rather than for any intrapsychic difficulty of his own. Then, like the good mother accompanying her child into a phobically regarded situation, his wife may come with him to conjoint therapy.

His wife's presence renders the sessions somewhat safer, but even so, they are likely initially to be fraught with anxiety for him. It is difficult for him to relax, to permit his feelings to surface and flow so that he might report them. Instead, we see him being practical, laying out the problem in explicit, concrete terms so that it is capable of what he would consider a rational solution.

The husband does not often choose to avail himself of the option of a different therapist, although he may have some uneasiness that his wife's therapist will side with her. Rather, he expresses a degree of connectedness and relative comfort with someone "who already knows the situation." His task-orientation leads him to declare it more efficient not to have to start afresh. Yet, of course, he senses the already existent rapport between the therapist and his wife, and is uneasy that they seem to share a language which he does not fully comprehend. His way of coping with this will be reflective of his ways of coping generally with an onslaught of feelings which are too much for him.

Sometimes he will directly challenge the therapist and her mode of working, acknowledging from the onset that he is a skeptic. One patient, a medical professional, said, "When a patient consults me I tell him exactly what the diagnosis is, and what needs to be done, and how long it will take, and the prognosis." He complained that he often left our session without the sense of a specific part of the job done. Thus he would have liked to impose his own instrumental ways, for they would enable him to bind his anxiety, to hold the line, to avoid the changes which his wife was wanting of him. If a man's apprehensions about emotional expression are too great, as in the case of this patient, he may need to withdraw from our mode of treatment, possibly to seek one of the many existent prescriptive modes on the market today.

But, if he is not too rigidly defended, and if the therapist can create a sufficiently "safe play space," he may permit himself to venture some explorations into freer ways of looking at himself and the situation. Although he will usually have presented himself as being there because his wife wants him to be, he comes to voice some complaints of his own, even if as a counter-offensive. If his wife has been busy kicking over the traces of the old housewife-mother role, he may begin by hinting that the children are somewhat neglected, that there's not enough food in the refrigerator, that he has to do much of the grocery shopping. Or, he may note that "mother" is no longer available to chauffeur, and that he finds himself driving the kids to Little League or Girl Scout meetings. He has less time for himself than formerly, and, in fact, is feeling a bit neglected.

Sometimes he discovers an envy of his wife's life style. One day, for instance, Mr. A's wife came to their conjoint session dressed for tennis, and Mr. A stated he wished he could be off to the courts too. Then, more seriously, he reflected how nice it would be to work just part-time, as she was doing, and have hours to spend in recreation or social activity. This led him into a series of worries and dissatisfactions with his own rigid schedule and with the sometimes arduous or boring aspects of his own work. She, on the other hand, unpressured by necessity, has usually been able to select a pursuit she finds absorbing and never tedious.

Often he would hardly have noticed how hum-drum he had permitted his life to become. One wife complained in a conjoint session that her husband almost never spoke with her about his work. His defense was, "What do you want me to do, recite the events of the day to you?" He recognized in his own response echoes of the little boy he once was, resenting the questions of his parents: "And what did you do at school today?" But more important still, he realized that his never sharing, either then or now, was in large measure because there was little he found fascinating enough to assume anyone else could be interested. Yet he had been a "good boy" and was now a "good husband," conscientiously and diligently doing what was required of him.

What his wife yearns to hear is something of what he is

thinking and feeling, not just what he is doing. Since, however, he has made a virtue of non-complaining, and since he has hardly acknowledged to himself the quiet desperation with which he often pursues his daily tasks, he cannot fulfill her wish that he should confide in her the workings of his mind and heart.

Noting his distress about her complaints, she reassures him that she feels his caring. She cites details of his helpfulness when she is needful, such as willingness to take time off to drive her to the physician or for other necessary tasks. But she wishes that he might sometime take off just to be with her, to play, to do something pleasurable. He acknowledges that life is relatively devoid of fun, with little time for levity.

Even sex isn't so delightful any more. It has become less and less frequent, and the quality is disappointing to both. If she complains, he feels pressure to perform, but this impairs his functioning. So she may give up her requests and approaches, and things fall into a stalemate, in which each views the other as a "stale mate."

In couple therapy the clinician faces two persons at probably very different stages of readiness for self-examination. The focus cannot be on intrapsychic conflicts, except as these are stirred up by the interactions of the two. Instead the therapist endeavors to enable each to hear the other and to communicate clearly his or her feelings and responses. If good interchange begins to occur, the man can jettison his former reluctance and experience a sense of participation equal to the woman's. The channel opens for moments of feeling with each other, for those mutual identifications upon which empathy depends.

Throughout, the therapist remains, as in individual sessions, essentially a catalyst, not directing or determining the interaction. She may relate her own observation when asked, and may alert one patient to reactions of the other, nuances which may have gone unnoticed. She remains non-judgmental and exposes any subtle attempts to get her to take sides by interpreting the felt need for an ally. Her role is to minimize the risk sensed by each in "opening up" with the other. When deeper exchanges begin to occur regularly and comfortably, the couple will often pose the question, "Why have we been able to do this here and why was it so hard at home?" The therapist then helps them to examine for themselves the prerequisites for that felt safety which enables them to work toward their goal of greater mutuality.

When both mates feel stuck in a sense of common stalemate, conjoint sessions may permit the discovery of covert collusions used as imagined protections against unspeakable anxieties about abandonment and severe emotional breakdown. Their primitive level of common clinging is based on an identification which can be recognized by the therapist and explored for both the threatening phantasies and the unconscious needs for safety. Then some participation in pleasurable activities may be liberated as a container for learning to communicate about feelings, preferences and wishes. Close to a clinical context, an umbrella of safety permits more differentiation and separation. Gradually, each may make a path to individual psychotherapy which can foster a flexible self no longer needing to survive by collusive behavior.

The success of these clinical processes depends crucially upon the therapist's ability to maintain an objective distance from the evident helplessness of the unconsciously conspiratorial couple and to avoid complicity from an attitude of sympathy, reassurance or advice. His own need to be helpful may tempt him to make useless and wasteful intrusions.

Chapter IV

A Special Kind of Therapist-Patient Collusion

The intimacy of the therapeutic alliance has traditionally been permeated with nuances of special secret closeness often approaching erotic involvement. The wish for help from a presumably abundant and superior source, a chosen therapist, may open one to a re-experiencing of some of the very earliest edition of such a model, with the given parent. Our basic thesis suggests that elemental needs are originally fulfilled in an emotional context of primary love which feels no measures or limits. Endless supplies, safety and right interaction are assumed and when confirmed, a free-flowing fusion ensues flexibly. This model is forever sought by us all. The challenge to the therapist is to so know his own resources and vulnerabilities that he may help the patient find her or his own way to remove obstacles that prevent re-experiencing qualities of the primary illusion.

The personal vulnerabilities of the therapist limit his availability for such ideal therapeutic processes. His inability to play or love well in his own life will obstruct his usefulness to his client's searching for better play, work and love. We present some case studies which illustrate a specially striking form of therapist failure to help, because of his vulnerability to erotic provocation by his patient or himself (Shor and Sanville, 1974).

Erotic Provocations and Dalliances

It has been rumored from time to time that some therapists transgress the traditional Hippocratic taboo against sexual involvement with their patients. Not only are these charges bruited about with increasing frequency, but a group of researchers has reported that one in 20 physicians in a certain metropolis admits to having sexual relations with his patients (Kardener, et al., 1973). Some writers attribute these alleged trends to a "new sexual morality," or to a new humanistic philosophy of wholehearted open relationship with patients. Others, such as Rubenstein and Levitt, blame a "why not" theme in our culture (Rubenstein & Levitt, 1973). Each of these possible factors is said to provide a rationale for the fad for male therapists to exploit the transference reactions of female patients. It has even been proposed that it may be therapeutic to break "this last taboo" (Shepard, 1971).

Freud, in his final *Outline of Psychoanalysis* (1939), concludes: "Real sexual relations between patients and analysts are out of the question, and even the subtler methods of satisfaction, such as the giving of preference, intimacy, and so on, are only sparingly granted by the analyst." However, his basic theory prepares us for an inherent ambiguity among "affectionate," "erotic," "sexual" and "genital" feelings, and he sees it as a goal of ego growth to develop the capacity for differentiation, refinement and flexible choice among these. Freud alerts us to the intrinsic complications of receiving the manifestations of these "positive" feelings. He recognizes the delicate difficulties of transforming such offerings into a working alliance (Freud, 1914b).

A symposium of classical analysts in 1969 reviewed the eroticized transference and other transference problems and concluded that "a considerable amount of work is necessary to de-cathect the substitute attachment and to allow a meaningful transference to develop in the analysis (Swartz, 1969). Among the variety of technical manipulations proposed was the suggestion that the patient be discontinued and referred to a female therapist. In fact, many female patients, both with and without a Women's Liberation argument, do come to seek help from female therapists, complaining about intrusions and teasings from their former therapists, who were male.

Freud, of course, used the Oedipal Complex as the springboard of his theories and described the therapeutic values of the spontaneous revivals of earlier trauma, now occurring in a safe context. Precisely because these erotic strivings are to be frustrated, our abstinence can evoke the crucial conflicts in trauma-like experiences of transference. Traditionalists have maintained not only that the patient who has been seduced by her therapist would not be helped, but that she could be permanently damaged, and probably incurable (Rubenstein & Levitt, 1973).

Ferenczi began his psychoanalytic career with a long period of orthodox practice, out of which he derived well recognized classical contributions. His later dissatisfactions with the depths of his therapeutic results led him to speculations and explorations which he hoped could revitalize psychoanalysis.

Psychoanalysis had traditionally emphasized the method of frustration (principle of abstinence). Ferenczi (1929) pointed out that it had also employed an opposite method, namely relaxation (principle of indulgence), especially in its use of free association. He experimented with "indulgence techniques" (such as manifesting a "friendly and benevolent attitude," extending a session, permitting the patient to move from the couch, an occasional home visit if the patient were indisposed, etc.), but always with an attempt to return to transference interpretations with their implicit frustration. Throughout he tried to be clear about the metapsychological consequences of the modified procedures. He was convinced that his "relaxation therapy" evoked a core of reconstructed past that had much more of a feeling of reality and concreteness than heretofore. This process, he hoped, might enable therapists to work with deeper trauma, which had not previously been verbalized because they had occurred in phases of development before "the organ of thought" was evolved. A repetition tendency could thus be converted into recollection.

The use of the two-fold method, of frustration and indulgence, requires of the therapist a greater mastery of his own character functioning. Excessive frustration can cloak unrecognized sadistic inclinations; and exaggerated tenderness can subserve hidden needs to provide corrective emotional experiences. Ferenczi emphasized that analysis would not gratify the patient's actively aggressive and sexual wishes or any of his other exaggerated demands.

Balint, who was Ferenczi's student and literary executor, was critical mainly of the therapist's presuming to know and prescribe for his patient. Balint believed it to be crucial that "the amount of excitation, the degree of tension" be determined "by the patient himself." Ferenczi's neglect of this he saw as responsible for "otherwise useful interventions . . . remaining ineffectual" (Balint, 1952).

Proceeding with this essential principle of self-determination, Balint discovered the clinical phenomena of a "benign regression" to "the new beginning" (Balint, 1952; 1959; 1968). After the analysis of "paranoid and depressive anxieties," then "the level of gratification never goes beyond that of mild forepleasure . . . *to a tranquil sense of well-being.*" Some of the clinical vignettes will illustrate the delicate and difficult issues in this perspective.

We have recently examined this Ferenczi-Balint concern with "benign regression" and have derived two principles of reparative regression (see Appendix B). Regressions are seen as spontaneously occurring "non-rational, non-reflective phases" of the treatment process which afford rich clinical possibilities, provided that the therapist is prepared with adequate theory, with appropriate clinical methods, and with a deeply comfortable sense of professional and personal ethics.

Our view is that the therapist who perceives the erotic provocations of his patients as genital is misinterpreting the cues. The patient is expressing deprivations or conflicts from a stage of life long preceding even the physical maturation of the genitals. The sexual provocations mask pre-oedipal problems which must be recognized and worked through.

We do not agree with those traditionalists who maintain that, if therapist collusions occur, the therapeutic situation is necessarily hopeless, or the patient is damaged beyond repair. Our experience is that many can be helped. Perhaps in the past, those patients who overtly demanded sex with their therapists were "very sick." But with the changes of sexual mores, particularly permitting more sexual assertiveness by women, such diagnoses are much less certain. Moreover, even in patients who have remained largely at the "child level" there will exist healthy components with which to work. Indeed it may be seen as a manifestation of strength when a patient leaves a colluding therapist.

Erotic transferences are bound to occur, and there is no insurance against a patient's occasional misinterpreting some cues from the therapist. However, the therapist who is well versed in the rapidly developing theories about the pre-oedipal origins of many adult difficulties and who is comfortably cognizant of subtle provocations that patients offer will be more likely to circumvent sexual traps. Also he will be able to help to repair damage from past collusions.

In this chapter we will discuss three types of case material and the relevant treatment approaches:

I. Patients who report intercourse with a previous therapist who imposes his sexuality.

II. Patients who report that a previous therapist suggested, by word or gesture, that they experience genital intimacy together; a professional seductiveness.

III. Patients who request or demand intercourse during work with us.

Imposing Intercourse

Our first case is that of a 32-year-old woman, with an abject and dead manner, who had been hospitalized several times as "psychotic." She reported, quite casually, that her most recent "analytically trained" therapist had persuaded her to accept his gentle sexual ministrations, after convincing her of her deep and bitter feelings of primary deprivation. She dismissed these experiences of intercourse as not helpful, but continued to feel that her therapist had been a kind, fatherly figure, who, sadly enough, had failed her. She reported also that over a decade she had allowed herself a myriad of sexual episodes with a variety of friends and relatives. Toward these experiences, too, she was left with the same feelings of irrelevance, in that they never convinced her of her worth.

The new therapist suggested that her sad, benign attitude toward her previous therapist was as a reinforcement of her long-standing resignation about "never being reached in the right places." This interpretive theme yielded much weeping and active yearning for pre-genital recognition and stimulation. She once again expressed her wishes for tender attention and responsiveness from a significant adult as confirmation of her own early self-worth and strivings. The therapist accepted the pre-oedipal projection, in a way similar to that recently prescribed by Kohut; that is, he allowed some temporary idealization of himself as a pre-genital source. The patient came gradually to reach for warm acceptance in the therapist's mirroring eyes. He, on his part, offered a friendly reflection of her specific reparative wishes and of the obstructive defenses that were encountered in the working through process.

A second case, a 30-year-old woman, also somewhat "dead," told of being dismissed by her former therapist when she remained numb to his sexual intrusions, as well as to his verbal interventions. She began her new therapy in a state of malignant regression, with a terror manifested by a protracted period of paralyzed silence. Her protectiveness of her puny sense of self was relieved after 18 sessions, during which the therapist offered his detailed speculations as to why she would not talk, and also confided to her his own cycles of effort, fatigue, mild annoyance and even moments of indifference, honestly admitting his powerless position. His openness allowed her to replace her fearful fantasies with substantial knowledge of his real "insides." When the patient was convinced of the safety of this new therapeutic situation, she began to verbalize her difficulties and gradually became ready for the mirroring transference (Kohut, 1971). In retrospect, the patient's feelings of benign regression became possible because of the therapist's evident efforts and flexibilities, offered in a non-intrusive but resourceful spirit, a model of interaction which illustrates some essential dynamics of Balint's concept of "primary love" (Balint, 1952; 1959; 1968).

Professional Seductiveness

What are the vicissitudes of therapy when the male therapist recommends to his female patient that intercourse with him would be of educational or therapeutic value?

A depressive and somatizing housewife came to the female co-author because of acute disappointment in her previous, rather extensive therapy. Originally she had sought treatment because of her utter lack of gratification in marriage. She felt that "the doctor tried to adjust" her to her marital circumstances, since she agreed that her husband was a good provider, "successful," true to her, and "well meaning." The previous therapist had worked toward the goal of her greater acceptance of her "fate in life," evidently hoping that she would come to feel more content. He had also tried to involve her husband, who, however, was willing to come to consultations only sporadically (Sanville & Shor, 1973). A stalemate occurred, neither patient nor therapist perceiving any improvement. It was then that the physician proposed that they "have an affair."

At first, she was titillated by the idea, and for some weeks engaged in many phantasies of him as her potential lover. It was to some extent the discrepancy between her imaginings and what she felt when actually with him that lead her to decline his suggestions. She perceived no love in his advances, only a clinical prescription. Thus, she concluded, nothing would be improved by agreeing to his proposition.

The new therapist started with a different premise, that this patient need not remain in or "adjust to" her marriage, but might create a different existence through development of some of her own inner resources. She came to recognize the meager sense of self fostered by both husband and doctor. Only after months of review of her involvement with the previous therapist could she come to see the essential strength manifested in her own decision to decline an affair. She saw basic similarities in how these two men had regarded her. The persisting element of disappointment and mourning deepened into a search for the origins of her tendency to self-denigration. The slow careful efforts in this new direction worked to fortify her feelings of initiative and independence. She separated from her husband, is now studying to be a secretary, and is living in an apartment of her own. She has not complained of her former physical symptoms.

Perhaps the explicitness of the former male therapist's offer allowed for the later exploration of her private contribution to the therapeutic stalemate. She could explore her phantasy yearnings, which were much like those of a little girl teased by her father; but, also like the little girl, she recognized her consequent feelings of being small and inadequate, not ready for genitality.

When the therapist's manner contains seductive gestures, we would seem to have a more difficult fault to repair. Here, of course, we must remember that patients' reports of non-verbal sexual provocations may contain projections and other distortions. Moreover, therapists' styles of expression vary, perhaps even with their changing moods. The ambiguities in communication are, of course, part of the rationale for the traditional character of the reserved, impersonal analyst. As therapists, we are somewhat at the mercy of the patient's interpretation of our natural expressive behavior. With the currently developing appreciation of the pre-verbal and non-verbal aspects of relationships, we are enabled to exercise a heightened awareness about our impact on the patient. And yet, these private reactions in our patients contain crucial determinants which may secretly complicate our work. Perhaps a case with extreme patient reactions will illustrate some of the difficulties present even in more subtle interactions.

A young woman in a state of panic appeared for a consultation, sent by a professional friend of whom she had requested a referral to a "female therapist." She was agitated, saying she did not know how to tell her problem. After nearly a half-hour of "beating about the bush," claiming embarrassment and mortification, she revealed that she had been in therapy with "a certain therapist," of whom she thought highly; and yet he had engaged in certain behaviors with her that she did not know how to understand. She insisted that she had benefited very much from her therapy, and yet it was possible, she thought, that she should now change therapists because she feared he was making sexual overtures toward her. On the other hand, she considered it possible that he had perceived her as the "hungry, needful child" that she knew herself to be and was simply being a kindly, warm, giving person. She said that he had held her on his lap, and had clasped her close to him on many occasions. When she phoned him in distress, he would come to her house, or see her in his office after hours and would stroke and calm her. Their routines with each other now included a "kiss hello," and a "kiss good-bye." In one way, she felt it would be the best experience in the world if he were to go ahead and have an affair with her. Yet, she thought, there was no reason why a man like that would want a woman like her, with all her neurotic ways. Such a relationship, she feared, "couldn't go anywhere," and she could even recognize that it might spoil the "something good" that she had. She felt that she was "going crazy" with this thing and didn't know whether to leave him or not. Throughout this discussion she had refrained from naming him. The consultant noted this to her. She then said that she hated to tell because she suspected that he was known to the consultant. She partly wanted to protect him in case he was thought "guilty," but also both hoped and feared that she would be sent back to him. Finally she told his name. All of the essential information about what was troubling her emerged toward the end of the hour, at which time she pressed for a decision about what to do. The consultant suggested another appointment since—although she seemed on the one hand to be asking for a prescription—she might be helped to reduce her ambivalence and think about it herself. She agreed to another appointment, but phoned and cancelled it through the exchange. The referral source reported that the patient had returned to her original therapist. No follow-up is available.

The case points up the complexities in such situations. Even the patient herself sees various ways of viewing her experience, and those ways are colored by her wishes and her fears. The fact that her therapist was known and respected added another complicating dimension. Although the outcome remains unknown, it had been the consultant's intent to enable this patient to reduce the panic which was preventing her making a self-determination.

The model which we find both comfortable and in keeping with our professional responsibilities would derive from two principles: First, we are never in a position to measure the *quantity* of those subjective forces in the patient which we may sometimes identify qualitatively in our interventions. Secondly, deriving from this, our only tenable position is to foster the patient's sense of her right and capacity to make her own measures and decisions. Our attitude is implicit in that principle of transference analysis which respects the fact that the patient's experience with anyone else in current or past interaction is never as knowable to us as to the patient, but we do have faith that the clarification of the patient's reactions with us will diminish her inclination to yield her autonomy in panic to another (Shor, 1961).

Consultations in psychotherapy can evoke temptations to assume a benign, authoritarian attitude toward the patient. We are here in danger of carrying over the medical model which appropriately accepts the responsibility of offering "another opinion." There, patients must depend on outside authorities for that information on which they can then make their own decisions. Such dependence on experts is antithetical to psychotherapy. Our role is rather to help the patient to a fuller awareness of inner obstacles to his own decision-making processes.

Meeting Sexual Demands of Patients

Up to this point, we have been considering clinical dilemmas when patients have experienced sexual advances with a previous therapist. In the course of a new therapy, it frequently happens that patients will discover how, in their previous stalemates, they might have been provoking and colluding. Such stalemates may even happen in the course of work with us. When we find ourselves struggling with the complexities of resolving such blocking, we can see how pre-oedipal forces make their impact in the guise of genital language and gestures. Some clinicians are at work in trying to elucidate these newly perceived therapeutic tasks. Yet, each of us has ultimate responsibility for identifying and eliminating his own possible provocations and collusions with patients.

In this new direction, we wish to offer some clinical vignettes in which some of our own patients have made direct requests and demands for physical intimacy. In these extreme examples, we illustrate some principles of theory and method which need refinement when applied to the more subtle provocations by patients.

> A sophisticated woman artist of 40, successful as an avant-garde painter, presented herself in treatment after a slight social acquaintance with her therapist. Her lover was a colleague from another analytic group. Her first sessions were sensitive, if guarded, reviews of her "rich and varied" love life, with no pointed urgencies or discomforts. When the therapist reflected to her the absence of any report of significant complaint, she began to hint at possible discontent with her lover. Then she offered him an appreciation of his thinking and personality as she had glimpsed these in writings and incidental social encounters. She expressed her interest in developing an intimate relationship with him, even now during the analysis, "to help deepen our work together." She asked directly whether he would agree to her plan. Reflecting her level of communication, he replied that his intent and interest were focused exclusively upon the patient's doubts and difficulties about repairing herself. He suggested that her "admiration," combined with her choice of a professional consultation to pursue her aims, might imply some dissatisfactions with herself. She demured from any self-criticism but reasserted her wish to be valued by him personally. He commented that, as a starting point for their work, they could consider what seemed an element of belittling and distortion of herself behind the effort to manipulate him. She "allowed for" this possibility and expressed the hope that her work with him might render her more valuable and desirable in his eyes. He indicated that he was prepared to work toward her better valuation of herself rather than toward her reliance on the judgement of others.
>
> She agreed to proceed. Lying properly on the couch, she recounted details of her personal and professional successes. Instead of complaints or free associations, she subtly painted a polite, exhibitionistic portrait of herself, occasionally glancing at the therapist for its effect. Three sessions of such behavior provoked him to report to her his impression that her ongoing efforts were designed to win his admiration, with her

underlying self-doubts still secret. She sat up quickly, asserting that she did indeed value herself but would be willing to continue "our work" if he would assure her that in six months or so he would venture an intimate relationship with her. He met her direct confrontation with an unwillingness to commit himself but with a readiness to continue exploring for any personal discomforts or complaints, even those in response to his decline of her conditions.

She decided not to continue, but in subsequent years sent him several patients. It remains uncertain whether the patient gained any glimpses into the sources of her manipulative character structure. However, she may have sensed in the behavior of the therapist, whom she admired, a less urgent attitude about genital intimacy.

This seemingly superficial and unsuccessful encounter may demonstrate something about therapeutic principles. When the patient makes a direct and strong verbal confrontation, it merits from the therapist a clear verbal response in terms of his own authentic and relevant emotional reality. This respectful reaction should be accompanied by his best tentative hypotheses about manifest transference distortions and ego weaknesses. Even if the patient does not then respond to our speculative interpretations, we will have kept open the path toward the essential work of therapy.

Another case vignette will illustrate our view that, when a patient makes a *gestural* demand for intimacy, we are perhaps even nearer to the underlying pre-oedipal problems. The act of provoking the therapist may be an unconscious test of his readiness to meet her problems at the more primary, pre-genital level (Shor, 1972).

A sallow, whining school teacher of 32, who had failed in a decade of attempting to become an actress, came with complaints about her dashing but neglectful actor husband. She felt a misfit in the libertarian theatrical milieu in which she had placed herself. For years, she had participated passively in "the new sexual morality" of her social circle, with little joy. And at home, she suffered both her husband's gross and inattentive behavior toward her. The early months of work yielded at first a deepened recognition of her pervasive and painful self-deprecations, since early childhood. Then a raging, greedy fury was liberated. The therapist identified the elements of strength in her new aggressiveness. She then began to express seductive ways toward him, squirming on the couch and verbally uttering blushing hints of her reviving

> erotic feelings. His interpretations about her delicate, fearful hopes to be received by him caused her next to direct her unaccustomed angers against him. Apparently she had experienced his serious attention to the shy and sly qualities of her erotic feelings as "teasings."
>
> At the end of a session in which she had been unusually stiff and silent, she suddenly got up from the couch and threw her arms around him tightly. She pushed her hips against his but her eyes were frantic and angry. When he looked at her with concern, she turned her face, pressed her head into his neck and began to make aggressive, rigid pelvic thrusts against him. His response was to place his hands gently on her taut and twisted neck, asking, "What is this bad and painful feeling up here when you also are asking for closeness?" She loosened her grasp on him and collapsed to the floor, heaving with sobs, her face contorted. He knelt near her, and when she had composed herself, she began to speak in a voice no longer whining, but reflective. She guessed that she had always used sex for "a little bit of body closeness." He recognized with her the importance of this realization and expressed his expectations that it would be of inestimable value in their future work. Indeed they proceeded for two years which were very fruitful, with no further provocative gestures.

Once again the therapist was seen by the patient as possibly provocative: he had encouraged the elucidation of her sexual phantasies; he had not forbidden her sexually aggressive acts; and he had in fact touched her. If she had left therapy at this early point, her story to a new therapist could well have aroused suspicions about the sexual maturity or professional ethics of the first therapist. The classical position has been that, when working with patients with "weak egos," we should avoid all three possible provocations. The fortunate and constructive outcome in this case may entitle us to some speculations about the many risks in such situations.

The clinical risks derive from an array of partially unknown, unknowable, unmeasured, and possibly unmeasurable forces. The patient, beset with wishes and fears and conflicts, is uncertain about the force of his needs vis à vis his strengths to prevent catastrophe, or his capacity to recover from a loss of his relative balance. All action implies some suspension of estimating and reflecting. In this sense, an act is akin to a temporary regression, also entailing, as it does, such suspension. A comfortable act both assumes and requires a safe context.

Thus, the patient may be initially insecure also about the therapist's capacities to accept and contain the patient's transitory self-attenuations, her "acting-out." She may also fear his being entrapped into acting out by her desperate pseudo-genital demands, in which event he would cease to function as her secure bridge from play to reality.

There are also risks in the therapist himself, his possible failures to attend to his own vulnerabilities and limitations in the face of the patient's unpredictable provocations. With this myriad of risks and ambiguities, we face great difficulties in evolving a viable working alliance. We have an ally in the patient's self-reparative wishes, which are hidden in the "acting-out." Perhaps a major value of the therapist's own analysis derives from his discovery of the reparative processes in himself. This enables him to identify explicitly the healing intents in the impulses and phantasies which have driven the patient to provocative behavior.

So far, we have discussed only the issues and risks between female patients and male therapists. This sexual combination appears the more prominent context for erotic complications. However, our deepening knowledge of infantile emotionality should prepare us for the possibilities of provocations and collusions in other combinations of patient and therapist sexual identities. We wish to present two final illustrations from our practice: the first, between a female therapist and a male patient, and the second, between a male therapist and a male patient.

> A highly successful actor in his late thirties applied for treatment because of his guilt and remorse following the recent breakup of his second marriage. He was beset also with doubts about his own adequacy. He began treatment by many uncomfortable comparisons of himself with his powerful and perfectionistic father. He referred to his relationship with his mother as more comforting and easy by comparison.
>
> One late evening he phoned the therapist and asked anxiously if she would come for a drink. She declined but offered him an extra appointment. At that session, he described a traumatic situation in his work. He was supposed to do a scene which entailed being photographed on top of a sky-scraper. With cameras and crew and fellow actors all watching, he succumbed to an old height phobia and was chagrined to find himself bursting into tears before everyone.

The others consoled him, and somehow, with a few trick shots, the scene was done. When he finished, he asked a female crew worker to have a drink with him and urgently inquired if she would let him have intercourse with her. She refused, saying she was involved. He reported with embarrassment that it was then he phoned the therapist.

She commented that his sexual aggressiveness was concealing his wish to be held and comforted by a maternal figure. He was relieved at the interpretation and proceeded to recall a related mortification. As a small youngster, he climbed a garage roof with some older boys, and all but he jumped down. He had been terrified to do so, and they left him there, frightened and crying for his mother. She did not come, and indeed often did not come when he needed her. She was never very well, and died during his adolescence. As this was worked through, he came to see in the sexual urgency which he often felt in later traumatic situations a regressive need to merge with a mother, to erase the boundaries with her, to keep her with him always so that he would not need to confront the masculine competitive world. He had felt the same urgency when he had phoned the therapist but he really wanted, he concluded, just to be held close and made to feel "good" even if he was not always brave.

A social science professor, who had had many years of psychoanalytic therapies because of his secretive homosexual practices with youngsters, resumed analysis in his forties. He focused quickly on his "reservoir of fury" against his puritanical yet seductive mother for double-binding his assertiveness.

Here only one clinical incident, an aggressive homosexual "acting-out," will be reported to illustrate some basic similarities, in dynamics and in treatment process, to the case described earlier of the female school teacher who grabbed and embraced her therapist.

On the couch, he fumed with a staccato rage about his mother's subtle, seductive criticisms of his boyish spontaneities. The therapist interpreted his vocal style, gestures, and body postures as signifying a deeper and constricting terror. The patient leaped off the couch and turned toward him defiantly. He exposed his penis and held it, erect, as though it were a weapon. The therapist stood up and approached him with tender concern. The patient's eyes turned fearful, though his jaws remained clenched. The therapist put one arm gently on his shoulder and said: "I feel you are confused, between your wish to trust me and your fear of destroying me." He fell to the floor, panting and in tears for several

> minutes, finally saying: "I had no way to turn and I couldn't just take it from her. I just felt helplessly impotent and sorry for myself." This affect-laden insight guided the working through processes. Eventually he relinquished his homosexual behavior, with its rituals which had always required that he phantasy or play at torturing the young boys he molested.

These two final case illustrations surely raise even more questions about treatment theory and technique. We could ask whether the "acting-out" is inevitable or provoked. We may wonder whether the regressions are necessary for a deeper therapeutic result. Would another interpretive approach allow us to avoid any of the non-verbal interventions? Or are there patients who must act-out in order to remember effectively? Can we agree about the advantages and manageability of having such "self-traumatizing provocations" (Shor, 1972) occur *within* the clinical setting? Are child therapists perhaps in a position to be especially helpful with these questions?

We have focused primarily on the current concern about male therapists and female patients in erotic collusion. One might expect that overtures from male patients to female therapists would be even more frequent since males are presumably biologically the more aggressive and intrusive sex, and our culture has assigned them the right to take the initiative. Several other factors, however, may be determinants in the opposite direction. A stronger taboo may exist against incest between mother and son, as that is reportedly more rare than between father and daughter. When a male patient permits himself some dependency on the female therapist, it may evoke the earliest images of relationship with a woman, and therefore be more ambivalent. However, following the oedipal period, he has been increasingly pressed to show his phallic adequacy. Thus, he may resort to a sexual overture at times to conceal his infantile conflict.

However, his sexual provocations are less likely to evoke a sexual responsiveness in the female therapist. Her concept of the therapeutic role may be more determined by inclinations to "care for" her patients. We have no reports in our practice of instances in which the female therapist had intercourse with her male patient, or even recommended such. It does seem to us that a male patient with a female therapist may more quickly come to recognize his erotic feelings as a mask for deeper yearnings, perhaps especially when the therapist is older.

The pitfall for the male therapist may be the chauvinist phantasy, which he shares with other men in our society, that he might liberate a woman by the gift of his virility. But there may exist for the female therapist another kind of pitfall, the phantasy of liberating a male patient by mothering him. If that mothering, like all "good enough mothering," includes a willingness to let go when the patient-child is ready to take independent steps, it may foster emotional growth and self-development. If not, then there can be a stalemate from this maternal form of seduction too.

Our data about sexual interplay between therapists and patients are understandably incomplete. But the clinical observations we do have all suggest the absence of any therapeutic value for the patient, and the presence of new personal and professional complications for both parties. Whether a passionate or a casual intercourse, for one or both of the partners, the underlying needs and the inequalities of the relationship come to disrupt the phantasies of fulfillment or even the pleasure of any playfulness. Such excursions are wasteful and at best expose the vulnerabilities of the therapist which make further clinical work with the patient specially difficult. Several of the cases reported illustrate that a basic repair and a renewal of valuable therapeutic work are possible by analysis of deeper pre-oedipal problems.

However, sexual collusions between very unequal persons have been traditional in many societies. We next examine such phenomena in our own culture as they become available for analytic investigation.

Chapter V

Playmating

In recent years we have noted that an increasing number of our mature women patients are taking on much younger lovers. In therapy they are eager to examine these adventures and alliances with their "boys." Men have presumed as their birthright to own, manage and manipulate young "girls," but in striking contrast to the new women, our male patients are disinclined to see such behavior as an issue for analysis and they are evasive when our work allows them to glimpse dissatisfactions and discomforts in such affairs or marriages (Sanville and Shor, 1975a).

Our thesis is that one promising consequence of the women's liberation movement will be the discovery and enjoyment of more processes of mutual experiencing. Women are experimenting and exploring the reparative values of self-conscious analytic examination of their adventures with younger men. We also see them reviewing what they had not previously examined, namely their traditional exploitation of older men. Such two-sided progress in insight may provoke a fundamental challenge to men to confront their own dissatisfactions with younger women. As clinicians, equipped with new theories and methods for analyzing difficulties originating in the first years of life, we can now work beyond the classical oedipal explanations. We are able to identify the dynamics of primary trauma: deprivations (oral), suppressions (anal), and frustrations (phallic).

The case examples will illustrate reparative processes in some patients. First we will look at males who, provoked by their women, are beginning to examine their traditional exploitations of the opposite sex. Then we will present several cases of women experimenting in affairs with younger men, and learning through their treatment the limitations of such exploits. Finally, we will venture into some tentative predictions about coming phases of interaction between liberated men and women in their search for patterns of mutual fulfillment.

Older Men—Young Girls

Our first illustration is of a man from a very traditional background, fifty-five years of age, successful in business, divorced for some ten years. He came to treatment with diffuse complaints about his unsatisfactory love life. He reported no problems of potency, and no lack of sexual playmates. He was referred to the female co-author by a lover only a few years younger than he. Previously, he had consulted both a hypnotist and a behavior-modification therapist, hoping to be manipulated into expelling his "guilties."

With his first analyst, the female co-author, he quickly revealed that he had been the favourite of his seductive mother. Yet he somehow felt that her possessiveness had hampered his "development." He blamed her for rejecting his one "true love," whom he had hoped to marry thirty years ago. He later submitted to a more "acceptable" marriage prospect and endured ten years with his wife, allowing a large family to happen in tolerance of their religious principles. He gave few details of his current program of heterosexual activity, except for his ambivalent attachment to the woman who referred him. Rather, he related assorted memories of childhood sexuality, adolescent homosexual incidents, and later perversions. With the female therapist he played the good little boy making confessions, but in fact substantially eluding any examination of his current promiscuity. He teasingly alluded to secret erotic phantasies but refused to explore them. After a suspension of sessions, which was part of his evasiveness, he welcomed the suggestion that he might work with a male therapist.

Very quickly he adopted the new therapist as the good father who might "teach" him to enjoy life. He soon admitted wishes to be led by the hand to overcome his feelings of worthlessness, emptiness and boredom. He now spoke easily, even glibly of his almost compulsive sexual indulgence with women twenty to thirty years his junior, reporting his daily dilemma as to which young girl he would call for the evening's playful episode. Despite his confident managing of these "affairs," he regularly became bored, and felt empty. So he continued the controlled relationship with the one near-age mate, with anxious concern that he might lose her completely. He sees her as more intelligent, helpful and resourceful. While he would not tell her about his adventures with young girls, he hounded her into confessing any possible infidelity on her part. It was only when she made such admissions that he could feel the pain in his own "guts."

In therapy, he was led to recognize his provocations to her infidelities, and to confront those self-doubts which had made it necessary that he seek out immature women. His testing of his "superior girlfriend" contains the hope that this "source" will supply him well enough and yet encourage his moves toward confident independence instead of teasing him and burdening him with an unsatisfied older woman as his mother had done. He has begun to project this conflict into the transference with a resulting oscillation between resistance and persistence in working through.

Certain details of his comparative sexual experiences may be crucial to our thesis. His near contemporary lover tells him that he alone has succeeded in giving her an orgasm. While he prizes this special hold over her, he becomes increasingly worried that she might discard him because of his secretiveness and his avoidance of commitment. Although he holds her at some distance, nevertheless he privately phantasizes that "somehow" they too will eventually live together forever. He remains indifferent as to whether his "goody" girls are sexually satisfied, and he prefers to avoid eye to eye intimacy with them, especially in bed. He easily claims his right to ejaculation when he wishes, although he is often content simply to cuddle with a warm body. Such indulgence had been granted him by his mother but had frightened him as he sensed her implicit sexual demands.

His insensitivity and his innocent manner with young girls is in striking contrast to his many-levelled concern about the significant older woman, whom he perceives as a basic source but as a potentially dangerous trap, requiring more than he can give. The clinical task is to help him to overcome such pregenital anxieties and thus allow him to discover and savor a more equal give-and-take. At present, he is accepting and welcoming phases of sexual abstinence while he reflects on the intra-psychic aspects of his dissatisfactions. So far he is struggling with his fear that a committed relationship would prevent his playing freely and developing autonomous interests and skills. Even with the therapist, he is ever wary about being controlled, and this is expressed in his requiring special arrangements in scheduling interviews. Consistent attention is necessary to his dual image of the therapist as a guiding parent, yet as possibly constricting and belittling.

Our second case is that of a more sophisticated man, whose experiences of these dilemmas are profound and painful, both in daily life and in the transference.

Mr. N, another successful man in his mid-fifties, was referred to the female co-author by a male analyst with whom he had worked for many years. The patient reported that he had made tremendous gains, particularly in overcoming his previous tendency to be chronically angry. However, his love life remained unsatisfactory, and his former analyst thought that he might benefit from working with a woman. Following his divorce from a wife to whom he had been married for eighteen years, he had had a number of affairs, one of which culminated in his living with a woman for the past two years. He made no point of her being thirteen years younger than he, but he complained of her inability to engage in equal dialogue with him, conversationally or sexually. She could barely comprehend his intellectual offerings and she was unable to respond orgasmically to him. The appeal which she exerted was complex. He liked her appearance and her manner of dress, for he enjoyed showing her off. But most of all he felt rewarded by the fact that this hostile, "man-hating" woman found him to be "different" from all other males, warm and caring. Early in his new therapy he brought in a playful cartoon she had drawn of herself with an enormous erect penis, and underneath, the inscription, "Helen loves Howard."

This led him into the earliest remembered experiences with his mother, who was forever giving him enemas, "fucking me in the rear." He recalled pleading with her to use the smaller syringe, and she would never do that—"but would fill me so full that I feared I would burst." When he chose, as he always had, women in some way maimed by early experiences with men, he felt safer, and could try to "repair" them. Although he yearned for a woman with whom there could be sharing, he was afraid lest such a woman be more powerful than he. In the transference, he frequently could not allow "in" the comments of the therapist, and his defenses against his fears of her strength were manifest in phantasies of raping her. Thus he recognized his use of sexuality for safety and conquest, not for mutual tenderness.

He had anxieties and guilts when he contemplated leaving his mistress, and so he offered to pay for her to have therapy. He had two possible outcomes in mind: preferably that the analyst might succeed in making her into the woman he wanted, but if that failed, would help her to endure the trauma of separation. She was referred to the male co-author.

Helen began her treatment with an appreciation of the "especially gentle qualities" in her sensitive lover. After her own divorce, she had had a decade of young men whom she managed casually in order to experience some power, in contrast to the baby doll role she had learned from her father's pressures and from her mother as a model. Her affairs with "boys" were hardly loving or mutual; she had neither the capacity nor the wish for mutuality during that period. Now she was hoping to be deeply valued by Howard, but she felt equipped only to serve him in the old traditional feminine ways. While he appreciated this servicing, his higher aims allowed him to preserve a manageable emotional distance from her; he remained defended.

Helen's first month of work with her therapist helped her to recognize the pain of her submissiveness, of having fallen into the same old "little girl trap." She came to feel the double bind inherent in accepting Howard's financial help for treatment, for he was both lover and father. She could see too that this confusion of roles did not permit her to enjoy him fully or to be a real "playmate." She became more alert to his straining at the leash of their relationship, with his real and neurotic dissatisfactions with her, and she prepared herself to give him his freedom. She co-operated in his "temporary" move from her house and then declared to him that she would not go back to their old way of relating anymore, "although I don't know what I'm going to do about myself." She has suspended treatment, saying that she wishes to get on her own feet financially.

Howard found his first weeks apart uneasy ones and yet resisted the pulls back to Helen. He missed having a woman to keep house for him, and he also felt he still needed the sexual outlet. He had phantasies about several young girls. He related a dream in which his son brought him a girl who took him to her bed, but in an adjacent bedroom were her parents. Although they seemed not to be judging at all, he "could not go through with it" there. He took her to his car, but "the car continued to roll" so no intercourse occurred. The parents he first identified as the therapist, but then recognized his own projection, the parents as part of himself: now not really disapproving, but viewing the situation as "unsuitable." The rolling car was himself, the self that wanted to "move on" and not be stuck with another regressive stance. In fact, he has been enduring a temporary period of sexual abstinence rather than "move backward."

He permitted himself phantasies about his therapist, but then would reign himself in, saying, "But you are too old for me" (she being just his age). He tried to project onto her his own discomforts with choices of girls because of their beauty or their youth. But over and over, he had to deal with the freedom which the analytic situation restores, and hence to confront his own old tendencies to frustrate himself by choosing "safe" women—either "children" to be brought up or damaged ones to be repaired. Dreams continue to illustrate his dilemma. For example, a recent one was of finding a bowl of pears and selecting a greenish one, only to find that an "overripe" one with a slightly blotched skin was in fact sweeter and juicier.

A series of painful episodes generally punctuates the parting of playmates. Howard, for example, continued to give Helen a check for her therapy, and always deposited this personally in her mail box. On a recent occasion she phoned him to thank him but indicated that she could not accept his check as she had ceased therapy. She invited him to dinner, and he accepted. He reported that while he was there, her current young lover, "a tall blond child," appeared at the door, saying he had forgotten his breakfast cereal. Helen had been embarrassed, apologized for this "foolish kid," assured Howard that the lad "meant nothing" to her. Howard, however, described to his therapist his disappointment and even disgust that she should "carry on" with a youngster. When the therapist quietly noted that the same age difference pertained between him and Helen, he simply retorted, "But she is a woman!" He could not yet countenance woman's doing what man has always done. In the following hour he returned to look at the mirror that the therapist had held to him, and he is in the process of re-examining through the transference the hidden child aspects of himself. But the basic position persists for such anxious men: to play the child/boy requires an attentive and protective mother/woman, not a child/girl at play herself.

Many therapists have been reporting an increase in impotence among male patients in recent years. This symptom may be like the abstinence in Howard's case, a fresh phase of reconsideration of no longer satisfactory patterns of relationship. The final section of this chapter, speculates on the meanings of these and other manifestations of disruptions of traditional patterns.

We have presented these two examples of traditional masculine styles at different stages of self-liberation. In both cases there is constructive provocation by women somewhat advanced beyond conventional roles. Our next section will explore, from the standpoint of female patients, their phase of experimenting with affairs involving much younger men.

Older Women—Young Boys

Women are beginning to insist on their right to play too. The long kept child-wife now is claiming her turn at a phase of play-mating. Her traditional role has saddled her with a reservoir of resentment against being "man-handled" by her parent-husband. In return for his granting her dependency, she has had to relinquish substantial autonomy. Because she has known the submissive position, she can exercise her parenting with a more sensitive empathy than can her mate, but sooner or later her suppressed aggression moves her to revise the classical mother function. It is especially she who has granted her children those new freedoms which have characterized this permissive era, and now, stimulated by envy, she also grants herself some of these new liberties to explore life. As might be anticipated from her background, she tends to do her play-mating somewhat differently than did the older man. She carries on her affairs with a selfconsciousness which, in therapy, may lead to a fruitful selfawareness. She brings to sessions her dilemmas about her experimentations, both their possible value in her own growth, and the guilts that are stirred up by using young men for such purposes. Several case examples will illustrate these points.

> Mrs. D., a forty-three year old married woman with three teenage daughters, sought treatment because of increasing marital unhappiness. At first, she described a relationship that had been "idyllic" for years. Her husband had been devoted to her. Friends saw them as the "ideal couple." He had never been exactly demonstrative, but had been a "good" husband and father. In the last few years he had grown more and more reluctant to touch her, and sex had dwindled to nothing. She partly felt that something must be wrong with her and partly began to be aware that her husband's character limited the mutuality which he could bear. At her insistence he sought treatment too, but did not follow through.

Instead, he left her. Devastated for a while, Mrs. D. utilized this breach to note some aspects of the marriage which had been to her disadvantage—how, for example, in spite of being nearly the same age as her husband, she had really "played child" to him, depended upon him for many things that she had now to do for herself. She also recognized that she had manipulated him to give the responses that she needed, and some of the emotional blackmail she had employed, such as threats of suicide, she came to view with much self-disgust. She had never aspired to be other than a housewife, but now she returned to school and was delighted to discover within herself many interests and abilities.

It was at this point that her fifteen-year-old daughter brought home one evening "a nice boy" of twenty-one, whom, however, she felt to be "too old" for her. All of the family liked him, and soon he became a regular visitor. He was warm and affectionate, helped around the house. Several nights when the girls were out, he sat watching TV with Mrs. D, and would hold hands and hug her. Initially, as she reported all this, it was just to reflect how good that felt to have this affection seem so natural, so freely offered. She tried to quell the physical stirrings, but soon, encouraged by the young man's easy acceptance of sexuality, they were involved in an ongoing affair. For some months this was carried on secretively, since Mrs. D. was concerned about how her daughters would take it, but eventually he moved in with them. The girls, although admitting some complicated ambivalent feelings, did not seem unduly disturbed, except when the young man ventured into any sort of disciplinary role with them. They manifested much more discomfort with the fact that their father had taken in a young girl of twenty to live with him.

Mrs. D. has been clear from the start that she would not marry her young lover. She sees him as having ways which are many years behind her, modes of talking and dressing, interests which could not be hers, certain social ineptitudes. Her dissatisfactions have led her to take on the task of educating him in a number of respects, and like her children, he has sometimes resisted. Her sensitivity to that has led her to note an old tendency to mold her man into that which would satisfy her. She observes how problems arise from this confusion of roles. Recently, she has been seeing that to play the parent "somehow spoils the fun!" Although she is in the process of gently disengaging, she is resolved that in any future central relationship she will claim for herself that quality of easy warmth and spontaneity which she has experienced with her young lover.

When a woman with a background of a longstanding marriage to a man many years her senior proceeds to have an affair with a youth, it may lead to more disruptive complications. The inherent lack of mutuality in the marital relationship can result in a buildup of angers in the husband, leaving the wife with an enormous void to fill. The traditional father-husband feels deposed and is furious while the self-liberating child-wife throws judgment to the winds in her grasping for elemental satisfactions.

> Mrs. R, aged forty-two, was referred by her attorney who reported that, in a pending divorce suit, his client was in danger of losing custody of her three teenage children, owing to an affair that she was carrying on with a young man of twenty-seven. Mrs. R was at first reluctant to consult with an older woman therapist, fearing that her age would make it unlikely that she would understand. However, after a brief period of "testing out," she told the following story. She had been married to a man some thirteen years older than herself, who had supported her elegantly from a material standpoint. But he had consistently been unfaithful, and ever since she had found him in bed with her best friend some ten years previously, they had existed in a state of mutual antagonism. She was resistant to his sexual overtures, and from time to time he was so enraged by her refusals that he virtually raped her. She reported these events with a degree of triumph, as though to say that such behavior revealed his essential bestiality. He was away on business a great deal, and while he was gone on a recent trip of several months' duration, she met Grant, a young, "way out" chap. Grant began to come by for dinner, and they talked and listened to the sort of music they both liked. He was warm and attentive and had ideas, new to her, about the rights of women. Soon they were enjoying an affair. When the children found out that the young man was spending the night, they responded by teasing their mother and threatening to tell their father. There is perhaps some clue in this to her egalitarian feelings with the children. In any event the lovers made no attempt to hide their relationship, and Mrs. R. defended this stance by affirming her right to receive in full measure what her young lover had to offer, adding that she did not want to go off from the children to indulge her hunger for this affection. It was, moreover, the first time in their lives that the children had witnessed respect and caring between a man and a woman. She considered that her open affair was far more worthy and meaningful than the many secret philanderings of her husband. Neither she nor Grant would deny it, nor

would they justify it by announcing an intent to marry (a move which, the attorney wryly confessed, would have made his task easier).

Mrs. R. realized the likelihood that she would be cut off financially, and that Grant was not about to take on responsibility for her, for he did not believe in marriage. To have a relationship of non-dependency she would have to "grow up." Thus, although the strain of the unhappy years had left its mark in the form of numerous somatic symptoms, she contemplated in her therapeutic hours a possible return to the world of work which she had abandoned at the time of her marriage. She began to reconsider what motherhood had meant to her and to acknowledge uncertainty whether she had every been ready for that role. Sadly, she concluded, their father was not going to be much better for the children, but she would probably need to allow them a freedom of choice.

Mrs. D, our first case, was somewhat better integrated, and did not need to provoke such punishment from her husband as did Mrs. R. She could estimate somewhat more accurately the "cost" of her experimenting, and could determine what she could "afford."

A final case, an unmarried woman, illustrates the presence both of old ways and new forays in the same woman at the same time. An actress in her mid-thirties, very experienced sexually, sought treatment with the female co-author, "to learn the secret of success in love." She had actually inquired among her friends and colleagues for a therapist believed to have had an enduring and "happy marriage." Her own experiences, by contrast, had consisted of a series of ostensibly passionate lovers who then inexplicably "vanished into thin air." The one lasting relationship, from ages twenty until thirty, was with a man thirty years her senior who substantially supported her and her ailing mother while he carried on many affairs on the side. Toward the end of this alliance, Kathleen had a number of affairs herself of varying durations and intensities, all in search of a more central involvement which she knew to be lacking with her patron. Soon after her mother's death, one of her adventures provided her with hints of fuller sexual expressiveness than she had heretofore known. But this relationship ended in her lover abandoning her in order to become "a flaming faggot."

At the time she sought treatment, she had taken a position as a sort of manager-protector of an aged and affluent man, no longer sexually potent. She felt respected by him, mothered him responsibly, and enjoyed an interdependence which was free of sexual exploitation. It would seem that in this circumstance a remedial hope had been evoked, with a greater awareness that possible defects in her personality had made her vulnerable to being used and then abandoned. Despite these glimpses, she allowed a fresh repetition of being rushed and then dropped by still another much older man. But this time, it seemed, she had reacted less helplessly, for she initiated several further meetings with him. Moreover, she was now provoked to seek therapy for herself.

Equipped with some self respect from her job, and the felt protectiveness of her therapy, she embarked once more on a rampant round of promiscuity, but this time she reported to the therapist her ennui with these largely jaded lovers. Although these were powerful persons in her profession, she failed in her efforts to enlist their help in her career, and became increasingly aware of the conflict between her two aims: the search for a true lover and her aspirations as an actress. Essentially unready for either fulfillment, she bought herself "a house of her own," in a spirit of adolescent defiance, coupled with anxiety about her capacities to be independent, separate, and alone.

One of the furniture movers, a boy of nineteen, offered to stay on and help her with sorting and putting away her belongings. She welcomed Mike's offer out of gratitude for his practical assistance, appreciation of his friendly manner, and out of her fear of sleeping alone in her new house. She adopted this playmate as a fresh and precious sexual partner—as she herself had been more than fifteen years earlier. In numerous ways she saw herself reversing roles in her handling of him, caught herself repeating in detail certain condescending and teasing behaviours which she had suffered from her older lover. And she noted the origins of such meanness in her impatience with his childishness. She reigned herself in, indulged him as she had wished to be indulged. She even groomed him in fancy clothes and introduced him to producers and directors, aiming—as she had wished some of her lovers to aim—to make a star of him!

Her affair has lasted nearly a year. Although for some months she has felt an impatience to be rid of him, she has found it difficult to mean her often repeated "goodbyes." He is irresponsible and makes it increasingly evident that he is exploiting her, but he is fun. Against the heavy demands of caring for the old man, whose increasing crochety quality makes him more and more like a child, she feels the need for those carefree moments which she enjoys with Mike. But his frequent letting her down sends her scurrying back to some of the fathering of which her aged charge is still capable.

If one were to draw a cartoon of her plight at this phase in her development, it would be of a woman in superwoman's stance, stretching on the one hand to prevent an ancient fellow from being pulled by Death into his grave, and on the other, straining to prevent a juvenile lad from his avid pursuit of the divergent attractions of Life! In the process, we see the lady nearly torn asunder. The parenthetical subscript might read, "But when do I get mine?" This patient is beginning to feel that she must "divorce" them both if she is ever to find in one relationship that combination of qualities which she needs and wants. She realizes that to strive for that, she will need greater inner strength before she can consistently enjoy a truly rewarding playmate.

Juggling Intimacy and Autonomy

The struggle to balance sharing and individuality is manifest in two additional clinical vignettes.

A forty-year-old male actor avoided marriage to "devote myself totally to my profession—without the drag of a wife and babies around my neck." He maintained a career of middling success but skirted any woman who pressed him for a lasting commitment. He dabbled in psychotherapies, here also evading any intensive or continuous involvement.

In preparing for a major role, depicting a successful and powerful figure brought low by first inklings of aging, he suffered an hysterical breakdown while rehearsing for the scene in which the character must beg for sympathy from higher powers. The actor then returned to therapy for a more serious effort to work through his inability to play. He painfully relived his dread of placing himself in hands he could not control or predict. He utilized the flexibility of the therapist to feel safe enough and then learn the specific "regressive" wishes to trust absolutely, which he secretly nurtured. Thus partially equipped, he reached for a deeper intimacy with an actress fifteen years his junior. He felt confident he could control this younger colleague, especially since she evidently respected his talent as distinctly superior to hers.

He told her his strong wish for a quiet home base with the woman ever attentive to meeting his private domestic needs. She revered his lordly image and even promised explicitly that she would give up her career and not become pregnant for at least three years if he would marry her. Three months after the marriage ceremony, he learned that she had secretly resumed some minor professional activity outside their home, and he confronted her in fury. Her reply was innocent:

"I was so absolutely in love with you I would promise you anything but I expected that in return for that love you would soon be willing for me to play a little. We have so much time now."

His sense of aging sharpened his urgency about time and about hope for being given his period of total attention by an abundant source. He had yet to experience a deeper edition of the primary illusion in his therapy before he could know a more flexible responsiveness in himself and in his object of choice.

One final case illustration may suggest how a younger generation of playmates are exploring for a fuller sharing of both the "real" world of daily involvements and the illusion of absolute mutuality. Yet they too discover the infinite and painful possibility of personal differences as a challenge to sharing their individual paces of development. They each must confront, in a spiral of sensitivities, their wishes for a satisfactory oscillation between mutuality and autonomy.

A woman in her late twenties was living with a male colleague six years her junior. Both were employed in a specialized area of education which each had chosen prior to their meeting. Their common interests consolidated a bond which helped them to transcend many tensions from their divergent cultural, religious, economic and social backgrounds. They willingly gave up old friends and family connections in a spirit of planning together a fresh way of life based on a very private closeness to be enriched by the special professional concerns and ambitions each had selected.

The woman came to therapy after a year of living with her younger lover with the complaint that he had been pressing her to report in detail all of her sexual experiences prior to their meeting and then attacking her for "submitting to the obviously belittling, inferior positions" she had accepted in those relationships. She soon recognized that she was allowing a similar imposition on herself in confessing to him the painful aspects of those past affairs. She then countered his demeaning criticisms by sharing with him her perspective about previous emotional problems which had made her vulnerable, and about her constructive use of therapy to free herself of those submissive states. She even dared suggest that he seek professional help to overcome his need for her confessions and his angry rage in response to her honesty. He refused to consider therapy, hoping that their relationship would cure him.

But his cycles of depression recurred and his own professional work suffered. When he fell significantly behind her in

> promotions and salary, his helpless anger moved him to demand that both plan to leave the state and begin afresh in a new area of educational work. She was shocked and she rose to the confident assertion that her special interests and successes were too satisfying to abandon and that she had no guarantee that their leaving together would allay his deeper discontents and competitiveness. She told him, "You want me to be the whole world for you—in bed and everywhere else. I can't and I won't try—as much as I love our loving—so much better than I've ever known before." To her therapist, she added: "There are differences between my life experiences and his. I'm older and I've had more time, for complications, and also for solving some of them. I'm not willing to give up for him everything I've developed for myself. I'll be very sad if he breaks us apart."

Age differences make for actual and symbolic gaps to be bridged by the primary illusion of perfect, timeless harmony and identity of interests. Such vulnerability in continuous relationships is increased when one or the other partner feels ready or driven to take new steps in his or her further individual development. Again, women are more actively asserting a fresh drive to revise their traditionally submissive positions, and "grow up."

Toward a Model of Mutuality—Some Speculations

We have recognized in our clinical data the reluctance of some males to relinquish their traditions of indulgence in "fresh and precious" young girls, although we note some hints of restlessness and retreat. There are men who seem to manifest heightened discomfort as they are confronted with increasing frequency by women in the process of liberating themselves. These frightened ones may need for a time compulsively to play about with much younger females but may now be less likely to seek lifelong commitments with them. They neither give to, nor take as much as they once had from their child-women; they do not depend upon them nor permit the same degree of dependence. They rather want to join them in spirit in the hope of renewing a cycle of life development and of wiping out the paralyzing accretions of their previous role playing. The braver and more sensitive of them may come to therapists to examine their affairs and to reflect on their inner meanings, even with women therapists. They report more phases of sexual impotence, premature ejaculation, and unresponsiveness—at first with shock, then with appreciation for the sense of freedom and of the ultimate value of the right to say "No" rather than to engage in their previous acts of pseudo-intimacy. It is certain that these fluctuations in sexual performance reflect men's confusions and uncertainties in this transitional era. When such men work in therapy on these manifestations in their sexual behavior, they can discern the need to retreat for repair of their damaged sense of self. Longstanding narcissistic deficiencies are uncovered: inability to cry, to laugh, and permeating dreads of spontaneous instinctual expression even in play. Such weaknesses have been reinforced by the instrumental and power functions exercised by males in the service of general cultural progress, a progress which now permits and affords a further repair and liberation of long-subjected women as well.

Our new men are recognizing several layers of hidden fright and despair. They fear the possibility that there will be no one with whom they can have a satisfactory give and take relationship. Then, they may recognize that they feel inadequate even to manage their own everyday survival needs, such as food, laundry and the various domestic chores. On the deepest level, they come to confront a terror of fragmentation, and emptiness. We as therapists are but recently learning to help patients to utilize their regressions in the therapeutic process in such a way that they may repair their narcissistic deficiencies. Then they may come to feel more ready for mutual relationships in their worlds of work, love and play.

Our women are of course far less reluctant to move beyond their traditional roles. They are restless but not retreating. Our female patients have long exploited their father-husbands and have enjoyed the protective nests provided for them, but now they resent having paid the price of a restricted life for that security. Their new but often undefined demands press them into a sometimes awkward search which nettles and frightens many potential partners. Perhaps less frightened are the new young men seeking to learn ways that promise more satisfaction than that which their fathers attained. Such pairs of innocent playmates, the older women and young boys, have as yet no institutionalized forms for societal acceptance. The resultant public discomfort is permeated also with private uneasiness. These searching women come to psychotherapy therefore with a readiness to recognize the unsatisfactory aspects of their adventurous playmating. They complain of the boy-lover's wish to exploit them financially, their need to be taught correct dress or behavior, or even, on occasion, their requiring discipline, or perhaps their failure to provide "enough" phallic supplies. Our women seem not to become urgent or desperate about these complaints and they feel freer than their male counterparts to put aside these relationships, much as children do in their play. Perhaps they have initially a more playful attitude, since for years they have been granted a certain freedom from the instrumental role, and the expressive role has been closer to that of play. Winnicott makes the point that play can occur only when there is a safe "space" between mother and child, when the child can behave in a way that is both "me and not me." In the early stages of their affairs with youth, we see these women able to maintain a certain humourous perspective on events; they both are and are not really involved. After a time, however, their ability to play in that context wears thin. The old protective space afforded by the father-husband is gone and they must take on some aspects of the instrumental roles themselves, for their boy-lovers still want to remain children, or when they feel sufficiently fed, they grow up and go out to play with their age-mates. Weary of parenting children and lovers, these women then go about parenting themselves. They promise themselves to keep in mind both the qualities and prerequisites for safe play and they busy themselves with the next steps: self-selected education and training along intrinsic lines of interest and consolidation of their means of effective self-support and management of home and finances. In these areas men are indeed more advanced because of their traditional roles, and women are reaching to develop these capacities in themselves.

The lessons women are learning, the qualities they are distilling from their wayward playmating remain beacon insights to more mutual fulfillment, in time pursued with less desperate anxiety and less self-distortion. They too are repairing the weaknesses from their traditional roles, also in preparation for more of those qualities of mutual relationship which we presume to be ideal.

As both man and woman discover and then reduce their desperation about traditional sexual roles, an enriched playfulness begins to permeate the cultural atmosphere and fosters freer experimentation with intimate relationships. The present chapter deals primarily with the adventures of the older members of the sexual pairs. We have been noting that these patients are beginning to recognize their indulgence in less developed playmates as stages rather than final phases. These stages vary in initial urgency, duration, intensity, repetitiveness, and in the degree of resultant insight. But we believe that a basic thread runs through the variabilities, an intent to become equipped for eventual mutuality.

The ultimate ideal has yet to be fashioned by each person and perhaps by the culture at large. Our psychoanalytic framework permits some speculations about essential processes of intimacy entailed in a model of mutuality. One of the authors has suggested that:

> "the experience of oneness in mature love, in mutual orgasm, is the product of a dialogue between two persons feeling essentially and comfortably whole and separate . . . the mutuality includes processes of identification, participation, and communication, all moving toward moments of psychological and physiological unity." (Shor, 1972)

We can now recognize the forms of disturbance in the attempts at intimacy as they occur between the playmates we have been describing.

We postulate the core wish for spontaneous, wholehearted feelings of belonging to one another, a perfect harmony that is effortless and timeless. The "bedrock" for such experience is the capacity for empathy, derived from the maturation of processes of primary identification (Schafer, 1968). There are, in general, intrinsic limitations to the attainment of complete unity, but there are special limitations when the age differences are great between lovers. While women are probably more likely to find bases for identification with their young men, our clinical data have illustrated that such empathy is impaired by the tendency of the relationship to revert to one of role playing, with woman once more the parent rather than the playmate. Men have obstacles to identification with their female partners, in that they have long defended their psychological distance by mounting chauvinistic pedestals. More deeply, they harbour fears of recognizing their own hidden dependencies on women, younger or older. Deprived thus of comfortable identification with one another, the playmates may then reach for bonds in shared activities. The hope is to increase the sense of connectedness by fresh experiences together.

Participation in the spirit of mutuality requires equal interaction between persons whose significant needs and interests feel similar. Although the woman may at first partake of entertainments chosen by her young male lovers, the "charge" passes quickly. The older male, who generally selects the social activities, continues to accept his young partner's presence so long as she simply accommodates to his public and private needs. When she begins to complain, he is shocked to recognize the gaps in their requirements and life concerns. Women in the process of liberation more frequently than males seek such clarification in verbal exchange (Sanville and Shor, 1973). Thus one or the other will feel suppressed and distressed about the unsatisfactory nature of their joint activities. The couple may then attempt to "talk it out."

Communication, at its best, involves an effort to relate and explain one's central meanings and values to a reciprocally respected other who will comprehend and appreciate one's essential thoughts and feelings. Our patients show special difficulties with this inherently complicated human achievement. These playmating pairs may come ultimately to such attempts at confrontation, but the results are all too often a failure of language, a profound frustration. When there is a degree of success, it tends to expose basic discrepancies in understanding and motivation about life at that point.

Playboy and *Playgirl* are replete with details of physical sexuality, while we have hardly mentioned these. It is not that our patients or that we are shy. They frequently report even the minutiae of their sexual play, and we, in a spirit of friendly neutrality, reflect back the implicit emotional tones of complaint: of deprivation, of suppression, and of frustration. When they are thus able to see into their sexual problems, they begin to translate their physical experiences into psycho-dynamic processes. They recognize the hidden obstacles to identification, participation, and communication in these play-mating relationships. Of course, some gaps are inherent in the age differences. Further clinical investigation of these phenomena may permit more precise hypotheses about the patterns of tension and accommodation between playmates with various degrees of age-developmental discrepancies.

Chapter VI

Changing Partners and Roles

While playmating relationships in the male chauvinist tradition may be expected to decrease as women claim greater equality, some new forms of intimacy are appearing which are modifying the conventional marriage framework. Statistics are difficult to establish but perhaps the numbers are less relevant than the seemingly sudden change in public morality, in the manners and styles of marital bonding and sexual exchange. Even the law reflects the new tolerance for sexual relations between consenting adults, and infidelity is no longer a necessary grounds for divorce. In this less authoritarian atmosphere, sexual experimenters are redefining the lines between rewarding playfulness and a casualness which disorders and spoils the qualities of loving intimacy. The old words for emotional involvement are no longer fitting. "Lover?" "Mistress?" "Special friend?" "Mate?" New names are tried, like "intime." No terms seem to hold, to contain the strain between the private wish for flowing primary illusion and the public need for labels and fixed categories and judgments.

Most innovative cultural development and social change proceed independently, apart from official fostering. Professional and philosophical pronouncements usually come later, following the brave and foolish forays of venturers who risk with their own impulses and intuitions to their own ends, fortunate and unfortunate. Efforts by some women to fend off establishment pressures have produced some gross exaggerations and caricatures which pronounce a more open battle between the sexes. But the directness of such confrontations may serve to put away the haunting ghosts of morality and of "science" which have prematurely defined limits to female potentiality and destiny. The analytic clinician sees little of the earliest experimenters and can only speculate in reconstructions about first phases in the exploration of alternative styles of sexual arrangements.

Today it is evident that traditional male chauvinism has become a burden to some men, as well as to many women. The struggle to remove the yoke has produced powerful pushes toward selective or specialized forms of equality like sexual swinging, open marriage, commune living and more private alternatives. We offer our impressions from clinical glimpses.

Swinging

A few wives have come to psychotherapy in a quandary because of pressure by their husbands to join in mate-swapping parties. These women uniformly report their first shock reactions to the suggestion, though they had recognized the unsatisfactory intimacy with their husbands. They relate the edgy, uncomfortable discussions at home about the proposal to "swing" with other couples.

The more shocked wives would come to admit to phantasies about secret lovers or new marriages; these women always nursed painful but private wishes for perfect loving with one partner but they remained passive and submissive to their mates and waited in silence for some magical transformation. These fixated women would often comply with the husbands' proposal for mate-swapping but after a first or second exposure, they reach to psychotherapeutic help.

Here, we faced their deep passivity and the split between their primary wishes and self-devaluations. They report a need for the inner strength which would permit them to say "No," and yet also a wish to explore actively their own preferences. They begin to work toward an essential independence, and even separateness, if necessary. Instead of waiting passively for the magical source, protector and love partner, they come to claim the hope for a rich intimacy of mutuality.

Those wives who showed less resistance to the suggestion to engage in sexual swapping report some curiosity about the erotic styles of other men. Not so paralyzed by passivity and secret phantasies of magical perfection, they had flirted with infidelities and felt less trapped by their husbands' sexual predilections. One wife initiated the discussion of "swinging" with another couple which included a man about whom she had long phantasied. In contrast, according to our indirect data about husbands' proposals, the suggestions by men usually were toward relative strangers. We could speculate that male chauvinism fosters a wider, broader range of possible sexual partners. The wives choose to stay closer to home, remaining dependent upon a supporting male, while they seek permission and tolerance for their impulses to expand and grow, through sexual explorations.

These less passive women do engage in the group sex parties with more alertness to specific details of erotic behavior. They have made efforts to introduce into their own home lovemaking methods which they have learned abroad. The women report much uneasiness throughout all these proceedings, anxious not to show too much pleasure in these excursions or in making suggestions to their husbands. One of their general character traits is the reigning in of sensual excitement. This cautiousness signified awareness of the tense gap between their dependency upon a chauvinist male and their urgency to enrich the texture of intimate experience. The focus on sensuous parts and possibilities is interpreted as a wish to repossess lost body functions and sensitivities and hence to alleviate depressive anxieties (Klein, 1957). "Cooperative" wives reached these deep levels in their therapy more often than did "shocked" wives who had greater paranoid anxieties in their profoundly paralyzing passivity; the latter were less ready to challenge, or even to manipulate secretly the traditionally superior male.

In our cases, we found little evidence, so far, that sexual swinging facilitates oscillation toward mutuality between the original partners of a couple. Instead new complications appear, such as tensions over honesty about feelings, over symbolic possessiveness and loyalty, and over personal privacy. These swinging experiences are appended to a generally conventional front or style of life; more time may be necessary to learn whether or how a new integration will occur.

Opening Marriages

Sometimes, instead of swinging as a solution to dissatisfactions with each other, a couple comes to agree on sexual freedoms for each. Usually, but not always, the pact follows the discovery by the wife of her mate's infidelities, and it represents both an attempt at openness and an effort to overcome sexual jealousy. The persons who seek our help regularly report limited direct value in this experiment, but their very failure may provoke further searching within.

> Mr. N., for example, a professional man in his early 40's, sought treatment because his wife was threatening to discard him. Married for eighteen years, he had expended his energies for the first decade of that period almost totally on building up his practice and attaining material security and luxury for his family. His wife complained increasingly of his rarely being at home with her and their 3 children. She felt the whole responsibility of domestic chores to be hers. When he was with her, his fatigue dulled his interests in and capacities for sexual intimacy. She began to express profound resentments about his neglect of her. Feeling impotent to resolve the problems at home, he initiated a series of extramarital affairs. Although he considered himself an "expert in deception," his wife soon found out and violent confrontations occurred. Each time he would be so frightened at the possibility of losing her that he would promise earnestly never to be untrue again. But, as he explained in therapy, the female world out there was "like a bounteous banquet table" and he "like a starving man." He was "making up" for not having been attractive to girls in his adolescence, and for felt lacks with his wife. He particularly enjoyed the beginning of each relationship, the exhilaration of meeting and coming to know an attractive woman, and coming to feel his own attractiveness. It seemed "harmless" to him, and he could not even see why honesty was so important to his wife. He was claiming his private safe space to play. Nevertheless, when in desperation she proposed that if he could not relinquish his pattern of infidelities, they should both have the right to sexual excursions, he agreed, albeit uneasily. The plan was that they share their experiences by discussing them with each other.

At first it seemed to work. Mr. N. felt relief from guilt, in that he was no longer hiding his escapades, and from anxiety, in that he was not living in perpetual fear of being caught. Moreover, he and his wife found their sexuality together somehow enhanced, more exciting. So long as their assignations were on the same evenings, it went well. But when only one had a date, the other, remaining at home would be tormented by fearful phantasies of being supplanted. It was the wife who became impatient with the arrangement, declaring that she preferred her husband to these other men. She called a halt, eliciting once more a vow from her husband to remain true and to work out their difficulties with each other more directly. It had been his violation of the pledge that had catapulted their marriage to the brink and sent him scurrying to therapy. He was in such a state of apprehension that he feared for his very survival, since alarming cardiac symptoms had appeared along with long-standing gastro-intestinal difficulties.

Several features of this case may illustrate the dilemma for males today, and perhaps for therapists of our persuasion. He does not seek treatment until disaster is at hand, and then he is "frightened sick" at his own sense of helplessness. He literally invites the therapist to set up a "code of behavior" for him, a way that will lead to sure salvation. Already, after only several interviews, he finds it almost impossible not to press urgently for answers, and he is attracted to other therapies which promise simplification and salvation.

Feeling deprived by the wife-mother, he resorted, as have many males, to extensive phallic activity. The substitute nature of the privation phantasies is revealed in his metaphor of the banquet table at which he greedily gratifies his hungers. He had, as he revealed in one of his first hours, felt literally deprived orally, for his mother had been a "health food fanatic" who would not feed him meat, and he did not enjoy her endless beans and rice. But we can surmise that it was not only her actual food but her emotional nourishment which he found wanting. For she was, as he saw her, so rigid and puritanical, that his only pleasures had to be clandestine, possible only by deceit and lying. It was shortly after her death that he began his extra-marital adventures.

His success with women seemed to him for a while to compensate for a damaged narcissism. It was flattering to be so wanted, so well received. At one point he asked himself what would be wrong with a whole lifetime of affairs. If such fun could be had in bachelor life, why was he so unbearably terrified that his wife might abandon him? He is beginning to answer that for himself as he notes that the vitalizing effect on him of the getting-acquainted period with a woman soon wears off, and the ennui is relieved only by a new woman. He is becoming conscious of a dread that there might come to be a boredom with the very turnover, and that not much peace is accruing from such inconstancy. If he stays with therapy, it might be predicted that he will recognize the powerful wish for both constancy and change within one ever-growing relationship.

Communizing Old Roles

Some younger adults are experimenting with commune living where sexual intimacy and even the parent roles are shared among several cohabiting women and men in a wider rearrangement of more aspects of life. It is our impression that these pioneers rarely engage in intensive psychotherapy during these experiments.

A woman approaching thirty came for analytic therapy about a year after leaving a commune in which she had lived for four years. The members were articulate and artistic persons, active in a progressive educational movement and related professional functions. She had helped form the group along with her husband and two-year-old child. A gentle, sensitive permissive atmosphere seemed to pervade the large house which the eight to ten people occupied.

The patient reported that she found herself choosing to be sexual most often with an unmarried male member who hung about in a specially tender, auxiliary spirit. She noted that her husband seemed to prefer another woman in the group and then that her child showed increasing attachment to the husband's new choice. These arrangements persisted under a benign tolerance and with some flexibilities. However, when her husband declared that he wished to be sexual only with his new partner, she became upset and developed antagonism to the entire group. She worked her way out of the community, leaving her child, who insistently chose to remain with the new "mother."

Leaving the city, she took a professional position about 250 miles away. There she met a colleague who wished to be given much mothering. They were living together for several months when she came to therapy. The patient reviewed, with sensitive insight, her deep ambivalence about the maternal role. She reconstructed her long-buried but painful eagerness to serve her father, a stern minister. His rigid possessiveness of both wife and daughter left the mother feeling deprived, suppressed and frustrated. Neither parent met or fostered the child's spontaneity or expanding curiosity. The patient finally left her meagre home, hungry and vulnerable.

The broader cultural atmosphere outside her home promised possibilities of a less oppressive parent-child interaction. The patient was able partially to sublimate her hopes in her work as an art teacher in a progressive school where she could exercise specialized and limited parental responsibilities. She sought a wider repair by creating a "better family" in the open community she developed but this "alloplastic" effort to change society failed her personally.

Recognition of her hidden wishes for a perfect home source and protection permitted a less urgent and less devious search and effort. The short period of intensive therapy helped her to re-establish a flexible relationship with her daughter and the members of the commune. She finds some satisfaction and much consolation in the evidences that her child seems able to experience the changing phases of her attachment to adults with less drastic anxiousness or resignation than had been the burden for the patient with her parents. She believes that her daughter will impose less traumatic distortion on the future generation following her. Might such defusing of the nuclear family be a part of the cultural significance of the commune movement for human liberation? A period of less intense, less exclusive involvements may allow a clearer view of the inherent dilemmas embedded in the human condition of parenting, that original "impossible profession" (Freud, 1937).

Toward Flexible Closeness

A professional man in his early thirties toyed for several years with planning to form a commune as a complete way of life. He had married and divorced a decade earlier and, since then, he was living with a woman colleague who frequently, recurrently, "slipped into" pressing him to promise to marry her. Sometimes he was moved, privately, to consider "trying middle America, the house, fine cars and things, the professional ambitions and all that." More often he preferred their current style of independence and autonomy; he hoped she would be a safe companion and context for his search for his own emotional freedom from angry dependent females, like his mother and his previous wife. He is hoping that his presence will also help his present woman to free herself of "the need to marry." Their relationship seems permeated with a sensitive spirit of tolerant patience for one another's tensions about marriage, their conflicts about a permanent legal commitment.

In his therapy, he came to recognize primitive sources of his fears of fusion, of sharing all his deep and elemental good feelings as though forever. When his mate would erupt into a tearful spasm demanding a legal tie, he would tease himself, and her, with new explorations into the idea of their organizing a commune with several close, congenial friends. Each such cycle yielded us further insights into paranoid-like dreads of being trapped into angry submissiveness and self-distorting compliance. He came to see, and say: "If I were able to join a commune, I could get married. It's the same problem."

He is recognizing a wish that each of them have a safe phase for reviving buried hopes to play freely and flexibly, to learn his and her own pace and measurements of wanting, fearing and resting. He had known his past efforts, and temporary successes, at compliant passiveness and compromise adaptations. He "could fake it." But now he wanted to rout out the hidden terrors which prevented him from risking making errors and learning from them. He is using his fuller awareness of his self-paralyzing phantasies to allow himself more separate experience of "owning my own energies," in solitary meditation, music and exercising. "I'll know when I'm ready for more." He recently reviewed his process of change: "I think my drive for mutuality has been too compulsive, a king of clinging. I feel a lower level of commitment right now. I'm less desperate to make it all work with her; first I want to feel more at home with myself, inside."

The clamor for equal rights, equal opportunities, equal time, is producing some gross, even grotesque caricatures of human relationship. Individual victims and victors happen, and cue in the rest of us for our more private struggles. But social and legal attitudes are changing on these matters; fewer medical or moral judgments or criminalistic condemnations are pronounced for imposed acts traditionally disapproved by a more rigid society. We have noted that even the official American Psychiatric Association, in 1973, decreed that homosexuality per se is no longer to be diagnosed as an emotional disorder. The battle for tolerances oscillates and mostly advances; and increasing numbers of persons reach to make their own measures and patterns to manage private impulses, pains, hopes and illusions.

Our working premise is that a universal primary illusion underlies the ongoing trend toward greater tolerance of experiments in "sexual equality." Most of us are becoming somewhat less urgent within our dark and difficult insides, and we feel ready to grant more leeway to the avant-garde who risk more than we do, while helping us to learn more about human possibilities. We suspend previous convictions and private sensitivities, as we wait with wonder and wariness.

Depth clinical data about these bolder explorers in sexual relating is rather meagre. Their patient focus on sexual vehavior per se as the cause of or solution to life's unhappiness seems to us a narrow approach to the rich processes which make for deeply fulfilling intimacy. But the proliferation of sex therapy today, with and without hired sexual surrogates, suggests similar panacea-thinking among impatient professions; here, the therapist is regularly instructing and prohibiting clients, contrary to the ethic of our clinical approach. Yet, all of these trends to action-protests may serve to relieve the social atmosphere of legal and moral injunctions against particular behaviors traditionally tabooed (Sanville and Shor, 1976). Thus more safe exploratory space may be created for private play and development later on. Meanwhile subtle personal sensitivities are suspended by these public, pressuring movements, perhaps for later revitalizing.

We see details in many of our patients of similar but spontaneous, private efforts toward freer sexual experimentation on a smaller scale. We attend to the reports of confrontation and accommodation by women who are reaching for conventionally male powers and positions in society and by men who are relinquishing controls and responsibilities at home and outside. We hear of new pleasures being discovered by each sex during their continual negotiations for revising the arrangements of home care, parental functions, financial management and the planning of recreation, together and separately. A subtler and more flexible pattern of individual preferences emerges when our patients uncover their previously unconscious role models and examine in therapy the haunting dreads and magical dreams which have molded these old models. Correspondingly, their sexual feelings, attitudes and behaviors change to reflect the new senses of self and of the other.

Our professional stance remains one of friendly neutrality, neither instructing nor prohibiting. We work to relieve patients of their projections onto us for responsibility and ultimate wisdom. New pleasures and new pains are discovered. The liberated ones complain of uneasiness about sharing everything, about being too honest, about losing all privacy. Many are ashamed of deep jealousy and fears of their lover's infidelity. The evolution of human intimacy will not stop in the present phase of change. Our assumption of open-ended growth must also allow for new equalities of distress and complaint to emerge, in a dialectic spiral of change.

Chapter VII

The Art of Parting

There are numerous versions of an old story which tells of an aging man recounting the many and varied loves of his life to a young man on the threshold. The account begins with the experience of a first date, with his fresh excitement about the quality of precious privateness and uneasy oppositeness in a demure yet emerging young girl. Our hero describes his overcoming the anxieties in the girl and then in himself, followed soon by a boredom and a retreat.

The next love was in a phase of sensual exploration, with the discovery of overwhelming genital discharge, and then the edgy but gradual accommodation of his sexual energies to a joint taming of his powerful surges. His enthusiasm abated and he sensed the belittled and submissive qualities in his partner. He withdrew in a mixture of shame about his performances and guilt about his exploitation.

The progression of loves proceeded through a sequence of conquests over excitements mixed with newly recognized pains, anxieties and depressions. There were fresh threats and promises in each succeeding love relationship. Each time he began with a next haunting uncertainty, a phase of preoccupation and a focus of effort. Each cycle led to the passing of his concern and a decline of interest. The series stretched through all the phases of his fifty years of intimate experiences.

The young listener to these accounts knew the aging lover

as a warm rich spirit, now in his seventies, with a vital and sensitive wife, two fully matured children and a number of lively grandchildren. And the young listener could see our hero's easy delight in interaction with all these persons. Puzzled, the visitor phrased his query to the old man carefully:

"I feel so very informed by your history of growing experiences as you learned to love. I see how beautifully you have come to live. I hope I will someday arrive at so full a place in life. Yet, when you think back to your many many lovers and remember how you later left them, and even were left by some, does it still pain you a little? Do you sometimes wonder whatever became of each or any of those once glorious persons to whom you devoted yourself, even if only for a short period? Do you try to imagine what your life today would be if you had remained loyal to any special one of those previous women?"

The old man's look softened and he spoke quietly and earnestly to his anxious listener:

"Yes, the ebb and flow of my needs has brought many periods of pain, when I felt isolated or empty, or just a total failure. I would sit with myself and ruminate about the immediate sense of collapse of my hopes. My confusion would hover over me until I could see how I had been urgent or uneasy at the start of that relationship and what I had been pressing or avoiding as we two shaped our loving and living together. Then I knew what we had done for one another's still dark places and we would look at each other with warm gratefulness."

The old man then smiled at his listener:

"As for those discarded women—that's no problem to me at all—nor to them either, I believe. All of them, the whole train of them, are the same person with whom I now live—my wife."

Not many of us are so fortunate to live through a spiral of meetings and partings at a pace so matched by an equally growing mate. Most of us must mourn alone our earlier experiences.

Mourning Processes in Constructive Parting

Since the primary illusion permeates the whole of life, it must contend with the conflicts and character hardening deposited in our depths during phases of defense against the previous failures and imperfections in loving. One may feel disillusioned, become resigned, either to a half-hearted relationship or to an endless series of superficial encounters.

We each emerge from a unique heritage of biological, social and individual experiences, composed by cosmic, spiritual and material forces which are still not comprehended well enough. Human evolution continues, as we increase our effective awareness about some of these forces and about realms of individual freedom of choice. Yet most of us run up against limitations which we feel are unmodifiable, irreversible. Balint has described the dangers of "malignant regression" when one is overwhelmed by the feeling of eternal restriction by a "basic fault" (1968). He also alerts the therapist to the subtle possibilities of creating a clinical atmosphere which may convert the sense of catastrophic crisis into a benign regression which can liberate "a new beginning." Then mourning over archaic limits or disasters may move one through the constriction of old scars, those trauma of deprivation, suppression and frustration.

The clinical process for such constructive mourning begins with the occasions of glimpsing primary illusion in benign regressions with the therapist. These tranquil states are experiences of perfect well-being, fully trusting that the analyst will respect the patient's expanding freedom for associations and for silences. Such benign regressions may be followed by a feeling of renewal, with freshly equipped efforts to repair long-standing feelings and phantasies of damage and deficiency. Also, the patient now may express a softer note of mellow mourning for the trauma which he feels are not reversible, including the injuries from and limitations of his sources. He may proceed with expanded hope and flexibility into his daily life of love, work and play, allowing and enjoying more occasions for regression satisfaction. These satisfactions approach the qualities of primary illusion, the effortless and timeless harmony, that were rediscovered in the moments of benign regression with the analyst (Shor, 1969).

Parting is a suspension of hopes for a complete experience of the primary illusion, but the separation may allow a fuller consciousness of these wishes and of the inner and outer obstacles. The haunting pains and anxieties in mourning contain a set of primitive phantasies which imply threats of total abandonment by others and fatal loss of one's sense of self, with feelings of emptiness, homelessness, helplessness and hopelessness. The emphasis and intensity of course will vary from one individual to another, or one phase to the next. The therapist needs to be prepared with a set of tentative hypotheses about the variety of specific types of loss which may be experienced as well as with a general understanding of the ways that special phantasy exaggerations produce the accentuated pains. The clinical task is to help the patient salvage the ultimate dream while relinquishing the specific attachments which failed. In unchosen partings, there is a deeper despair and a more complete disillusionment which will require a repair of the sense of self.

Every significant relationship will, when disrupted or dissolved, leave a residue of grief and depression. There is a wide array of current theoretical formulations about such mourning and melancholia: damaged self-esteem, self-hatred, "aggression turned inward," "Thanatos" or Death principle, super-ego punishment, basic hopelessness and helplessness, Existential Angst and Ennui, and more. Behind all these we see three essential types of loss feelings which may be activated by separation or divorce, by all partings:

1. Loss of basic supplies, emotional and material: feeling *deprived* of being loved, valued, given attention and concern in sensitive, flexible and adaptive ways; paranoid phantasies of abandonment to fragmentation and dissolution.
2. Loss of a protective safe place for learning, functioning and playful exploring of self and the outside world: feeling *suppressed*, in need of freedom for trial and error; depressive phantasies of isolation in dangerous open spaces or in oppressive confinement.
3. Loss of opportunities to exchange and communicate with valued others: feeling *frustrated* by rejecting and belittling forces; reactive phantasies of devaluation and impotent rage.

Each patient will manifest an individual emphasis and sequence of these sufferings, often beyond words. The sensitive clinician will know the times for keeping silence, and the times for speaking. If his comments help to identify the particular qualities of felt loss, the patient can see the specific strivings at stake and be nearer to redirecting his efforts and energies in planning.

The three types of loss correspond to failures at the three phases of maturation of human drives or instincts as proposed by Freud (1905): *source* (supplies), *aim* (functioning) and *object* (exchange). Recent analytic attention to regression and narcissism (e.g., Balint, 1952; Klein, 1957, and Kohut, 1971) has enriched our understanding of the primitive phantasy processes surrounding these phases of organizing and specifying basic wishes which underly meeting and parting.

Depressive patients are generally seen as presenting serious psychotherapeutic difficulties. The widespread auxiliary use of drugs testifies to the power of the non-verbal concomitants of depression, such as apathy and agitation. Especially when suicidal states and other malignant regressions emerge in treatment, the elemental unverbalizable layers of pain require, we believe, new ways of humanistic attending. The clinical task is to help patients to move from paralyzing body tensions and agitated crying to the concealed phantasies and deeper wishes (see Appendix B). These behavioral manifestations are communications to us of his stalemate, and so we offer our observations of his expressive gestures and postures, noting details of his muscular tensions—all as clues to the emotional significance of his patterns of breathing (Darwin, 1872). If he feels reached and attends to our cues, he can modify these expressions in an exploratory, near playful spirit to gain more awareness of his feeling tones. New memories and associations to the emotional tones emerge. A degree of distance and objectivity regarding his dilemma becomes likely and he can more flexibly consider reparative possibilities for his loss, even *new beginnings* (Balint, 1932).

The qualities of weeping are seen to change from a repetitious, agitated cycle to a gentle flow which releases the unconscious phantasies to an accepting awareness. The patients review the embedded stalemates, close to the now bearable feelings. Their softer sobbing accompanies the recognition of primary hopes for repairing of old trauma which had been hidden in the compromises supporting the recently lost relationships (Greenacre, 1966). They renew their wishes for the essential qualities they had sought. Equipped with a fuller consciousness of the neurotic phantasies and behaviors which had waylaid their hopes, they can proceed to reach anew, with the former partner, if they choose, or in new relationships.

The underlying urgency has abated, and the lesser desperation permits a freer, more flexible exploration with easier play and more effective work, with insightfulness. The patient will often leave us at this point, comfortably eager to see what life will bring and ready to make the adventure on his own, even toward unknown and unpredictable terrain. We do not outline or promise any specific patterns of behavior or relating. The client is parting, equipped with an alertness to his characteristic ways of confusing and distorting hopes and wishes. Such knowledge, in awareness, can protect and liberate both privacy and sharing, both selfhood and loving.

A Clinical Model

Here we focus on the principle of self-determining oscillations between reaching and withdrawing, between meeting and parting. This perspective is crucial to our clinical method of psychotherapy as well as to our theoretical framework about growth, development, maturity and "cure." It leads to modifications of the classical model of psychoanalytic treatment in which we were trained.

We do not require a fixed frequency of sessions. We offer our availability on a flexible basis, encouraging the clients' considered initiative about requesting more or fewer appointments, according to their measure of their current need for our presence and our observing and interpreting their functioning. Seeing the patients' good use of our elasticity encourages us to make our personal and professional lives more adaptable to the changing pace and rhythm of their wishes to meet with us, or to leave us.

Similarly, we try to prevent the patients' nursing a secret conviction that they should use the couch or that we prefer it. They will decide when and how they wish to free associate in our presence. In many such clinical details, we aim, especially through transference interpretations, to liberate more of their self-measurement and self-decision about reaching for or withdrawing from our attention and presence. Thus we never "terminate"; we never "close a case." The patient may do so, as often as he wishes; he hired the therapist to offer hypotheses, not to command, demand, persuade or pressure him from an authoritarian stance.

Yet, it is inherently an unequal relationship. The therapist should be "superior" in his emotional and intellectual readiness to attend non-judgmentally to a client's expressions and projections. The patient is superior in his closeness to the inner data which can make possible a therapeutic relationship; his is the energy which will power the reparative processes; and his is the imagination which will fashion the specific illusion that moves him forward. Until the therapist helps him to know these advantages, the client will harbor fears, even terrors, about exposure, manipulation and exploitation. The patient may flee or fight irrationally, both of which may be felt by the therapist as emotional threats and practical pressures. Ideally the professional partner in the relationship can better afford these dangers and therefore can serve as a model of integrity and flexibility in respecting the other's privacy and self-responsibility.

The therapist protects and furthers the working alliance by careful transference interpretations which stay close to the details of the experience shared in the session. Only secondarily and very tentatively does he refer to similar dynamics in the data derived from patients' reports about his past or other relationships. This existential ethic of the psychoanalytic method does permit the therapist, we think, to allude to experiences not shared by the two persons when these outside data seem analogous to the transference processes being examined. Thus our method is an intensive edition of the "here and now" spirit of much of modern humanism. Yet the analytic ethic offers a deeper and a more comprehensive existentialism if it respects the partings and the separateness which the other may choose at his own pace while offering tentative transference interpretations.

In *I and Thou,* Martin Buber invites us to delight in the spiritual processes of initiating every relationship, even every genuine human contact (1937): "All actual life is encounter" (p. 62). Buber has enriched the existential stance with a forward moving optimism about the potential senses of discovery and growth in open inter-acting. He recognizes the hope "to be embraced" in moments of intimate meeting as deriving from the model of "some paradise in the primal age of humanity" (p. 75). But he allows that "the individual has run its course" (p. 84). And Buber's humanistic existentialism finally stresses the "doom," the "oppressive" and the "deeper corruption" at the endings (p. 168).

From our view of the ongoing phases of development, we see a necessary supplement to the creative drive toward sensitive meetings. Equally essential is the complementary process of creative separating. Thus our dialectic may be: "all true living is meeting and parting." Each step in fuller relating permits a richer separating and autonomy, which then fosters a better next relating. The spiral dialectic can go on either within the same relationship or in the next relationships, throughout all the phases of human growth and development.

Erik Erikson has advanced the psychoanalytic developmental perspective enormously with his descriptions of the interactions between an individual's biological maturation and the cultural milieu, out of which evolve psychological qualities and ego capacities. These processes propel his now classical "eight ages of man" (1950 and 1964). Implicit in his view is the constructive possibility both of focusing on and then of moving beyond each phase of concern: first, with the primary source and protectors, then with narcissistic body skills and autonomy, with the oedipal parents, with competitive peers, with the search for a core identity. Erikson is less clear about parting with the later phases: private genital primacy, generative parental creativeness and finally a wise, integrative, serene, accepting maturity.

Our traditional Western distate for decline and death may explain the cultural resistance against any benign formulations about leaving the particular pleasures of full sexual vitality, or the fulfillments of parent-teacher responsibilities, or about the renunciation of physical existence and survival. The very recent flourishing of clinical and popular interest in geriatrics and dying may clear the path to a more flexible experiencing of older ages.

We have been richly stimulated toward such prospects by the free-swinging, yet scholarly speculations about the final, fifth or "leptoid" (leaping over gaps) stage in Gerald Heard's *Five Ages of Man* (1963). He foresees a new self-respect in aging when our culture comes to value the self-reflective integrations of which even physically flagging persons are capable. Heard recommends specific lines of neurological research possibilities of electrically re-energizing one's psychological functioning in this final stage of earthly existence. With such new resources, even the dying may be enabled to feel and express a message of gentle meeting and parting, in their edition of the primary illusion. Other pioneers have also begun to explore psychological, chemical and electrical methods for revitalizing the "senile" (Luce, 1970). We have yet to work clinically with many of these new oldsters in intensive psychotherapy.

Meanwhile, Erikson's concept of a "moratorium" in late adolescence is very useful clinically because it is highly illustrative of a constructive phase of retreat from social commitment in order to make a more private consolidation of efforts, energies and ambitions. Such a withdrawal from former pressures and positions allows a safer sifting of past experience and a fresh selection of clearer if narrower directions and goals.

More recent work by K. Kenniston (1970) has yielded an extension of Erikson's stagings: now there is in our culture a long phase of "youth," extending well into the third decade of life, and even longer. We see in that new stage also, a *series* of specific moratoria, occurring in more individual sequences of both personal, private dimensions and of public trial and error. These cycles may be viewed as spirals of preparations for next decisions about balancing intimacy and autonomy.

The early living-together and the frequent re-marriages now widely practiced suggest special efforts for refining intimacy while testing successive editions of the primary illusion of "forever together." Sociologists and journalists label these phenomena as "serial monogamy," sometimes implying a blind repetitive failure at real loving.

We often hear from our patients that previous psychoanalysts had warned them against new relationships because of fateful "character trends" which would only doom them to "repetition-compulsions." These analysts may have neglected to identify and illuminate the specific hidden reparative intents in the patient's impulses to do it again. If the patient gains awareness of the unconscious primitive aim for happy fusion, he has the impetus for overcoming those specific neurotic conflicts and anxious phantasies which constrict and compromise any advance toward his long range, even ultimate hopes, When people are equipped with such knowledge, they can measure more precisely their obstructive inner and outer forces. Learning can thus occur, beyond mere masochistic repetitions. In a later chapter we will attempt a fuller formulation of the clinical principlies implied in our emphasis on unconscious reparative aims leading toward the primary illusion. (See the principles of self-traumatization and self-provocation in Appendix B).

Just as all living matter tends toward physiological self-repair, so also does the human psyche tend toward repair from trauma. More complex organisms have a more elaborate path to weave through the dead and damaged parts, but they also have greater resources to redirect functions and transform energies toward larger networks of reconstruction. Man has evolved powers of thinking and imagination which, in consciousness, can guide the work of reparation.

It is generally conceded that improvements in human health and longevity are due mainly to public health measures which reduce noxious agents around and within the organism and liberate inherent self-defensive capacities as immunizations against falling ill. Moreover, intuitive physicians have always recognized that their patients' "cure" is more dependent upon intrinsic self-healing processes than upon medical prescriptions and interventions, which can only provide conditions favoring the mending. The occurrence of scars from past body insults and from psychological trauma continues to challenge therapeutic skills in maximizing patients' capacities for natural self-healing.

An emphasis on self-reparative processes assumes that specific models of perfection emerge in the organism as it evolves. The psychological model of the primary illusion, derived in our first chapter, can continue to guide in the clinical task of liberating such images and capacities as the person moves along his stages of development, through meetings and partings.

Leaving Without Parting

The formulations of existential humanism can encourage an optimistic spirit not only toward flexible meetings but also toward fruitful separations. As the improving patient regains his particular superiorities, he can indeed ease up the desperation of each moment of experience, the terror of disruptions of relationships, chosen or forced. He can overcome powerful phantasies of scarcity, oppression and failure. He may recognize further potentialities for living, aspects of his primary illusion, which he has yet to fulfill, but he can leave his present way of living while not parting with his hopes. He may leave therapy with a rich awareness that more work may be useful later on, with or without a hired analyst.

However, some clients flee in what may be a quick defensiveness, with a hurried front of optimism. It is not necessarily the therapist's clumsiness which causes the disruption of his efforts. The patient's terminating may deprive the clinician of ever learning either his own errors or the client's still deeper phantasy-projections which provoked the flight. This dilemma evokes several kinds of compromising reactions. Sometimes it is met with explicit advice to remain in treatment until the therapist determines that the so-called central problems have been "worked through." A less presumptuous clinician may sit helplessly in uneasy silence, feeling discouraged about his own method and theory. There are also professionals who muster their own optimism in a spirited summary of work well done; even such support may interfere with the patient's ongoing self-responsible progress or his full possession of his own earned advances.

Our approach is to continue our attentive presence and to offer tentative interpretations which focus on any hesitant or driven qualities in his decision to leave. We present the person with our hypotheses about his implicit uncertainties while he measures his own doubts and determination. Since the analyst's role is potentially interminable, like the wish for primary illusion, the patient will choose most correctly the process for leaving. "Since analysis makes possible only partial and one-sided regression it cannot provide the patient a fully finished experience" (Shor, 1954).

Each time the client leaves, he or she ideally feels more open to possibilities for a better approximation to the perfecting of the primary illusion in non-professional, private, intimate relating. Yet each sex may have special problems about reaching and parting.

Traditionally, the male more often seeks to control and limit the depth of fusion, though he expects the female to remain "true," and available for his return. Biologically, the model of male ejaculation may predispose him to leave the intimate meeting with less than primary loving. Culturally, he has been discouraged from yielding his autonomy and his power position to the dependent, clinging female who has needed him to be attached, even contained within, forever. This tradition has prevented a graceful oscillation between mating and parting.

Of course, long-standing socio-economic pressures have constrained women from protest or demand. Now she is moving to be freer, both to ask for more within a relationship and also to choose to leave temporarily or finally. She is preparing herself to be able genuinely to part, rather than just to flee or to leave under paralyzing duress. Social and legal changes are making this more possible, and the husbands of our female patients do seem to help facilitate such transitional processes even with the risk that their women may abandon them.

Those men who have engaged in intensive analysis do come to hope that more fulfilled, better equipped women will then be safer partners for their own deeper reaching for fusion in the primary illusion. The more developed males may have the abundance and empathy both to wait more patiently and also to provide assistance to females developing their instrumental capacities so that they may meet as more equal sharing partners. Similarly, self-sufficient women may offer helpful and hopeful patience to their men who are learning to enjoy expressiveness.

However, the social statistics remind us that legal separations and divorces are on the increase. And, clinically, we are frequently consulted by persons in painful distress about the dissolution of their primary relationships. The varieties of cruelty and inconsiderateness attest to the difficulties of constructive leaving.

New Manners and Morals in Separation and Divorce

Our cultural tradition has permitted the male the prerogative to modify his sexual arrangements in an arbitrary way. Law, religion and moralities have reinforced this one-sided indulgence in personal preferences. Self-questioning was not expected on the part of the male, and self-assertion was not tolerated on the part of the female. The first case to be presented here illustrates much of this old pattern, but with a few signs that, because the man is bringing himself to some examination of his inner presumptions, there could be eventual changes for both.

Mr. N., a professional man of 40, sought therapy because of suicidal impulses following his wife's declaration that their relationship was at an end. Married for three years, they had parted innumerable times, always following violent quarrels. On each occasion he would beg forgiveness, promise never again to be so cruel, but then compulsively would find himself doing the same old things, "provoked" by her. He now affirmed that he loved her more than life itself and if he could not "have" her he would prefer to die, and had so threatened her. However, he accepted the referral by a friend (who had gone through much the same story a few years ago) and has manifested a tentative willingness to look into himself. He told of an earlier marriage to a childhood sweetheart whom he had admired and aspired to emulate. After 15 years with her, he had become increasingly restive and had sought analytic help. However, shortly he had dropped therapy, "against advice," and simply moved to a separate apartment. He explained, "I needed all my energies to do it." In retrospect, it distresses him that he doesn't even know why he deemed it so urgent that he "get out," but there are hints that he felt inferior to his wife. After a brief period of bachelorhood, he met and pursued a woman he considered more ordinary, only then divorcing his wife. He married again, with the same imperativeness with which he had divorced. He suspects that he sought a role reversal, a situation in which he would be looked up to, and in which he would change the things he didn't like in the new woman.

So far it is emerging that the fights with his second wife were set off whenever she trod on his narcissistic toes by the slightest criticism, and he would retaliate by belittling her and her entire family. We would guess that these storms served to discharge venomous feelings, to achieve a separation, physical or psychological, and then permit a renewal.

Sex was always better following their battles; lurking boredom was dispelled and the zest of a new encounter was reexperienced. Mr. N., in his early sessions, struggled with an impulse to force himself on his wife, to move back home whether she wanted him or not. But he reflected that that would leave her no dignity, and moreover, that he wanted her to want him. So he instituted some dialogues with her, usually by phone, out of which she suggested that he come with her for conjoint therapy. However, he decided she was "too vulnerable" to take on this difficult task of self-scrutiny, and said frankly that he knows what is best for her. As soon as he had "won" her back, he declared he did not know what to work on in therapy, but suggested that he would like to decrease the frequency of his sessions to only once a week "till I see how it goes." He assured himself and the therapist that he would never let his wife know of his superior attitude "and besides, she wants me to be superior, to make decisions for her." Nevertheless, his own past experiences with being the inferior one in an unequal partnership may enable him eventually to see the problems inherent in attempting a reversal of his former situation. His wife has made him glimpse his past insensitivity to her, for she stated that she had had to leave him or lose her mind, and he had had "no idea that it was affecting" her so.

The therapist accepts his wanting to cut the frequency of therapy. She simply comments that he seems to want to see what he can do by himself, now that he has his wife back, and whether he will overcome a lurking uneasiness about the tendency to explode violently at any felt slight. The therapist believes that in his self-pacing context he may more quickly identify a next eruption of uncontrollable fury and resume intensive work.

A second case provides some contrast, in that it too involves childhood sweethearts, who, however, in the new mode, have not married but have lived together. In this instance, the patient is the female, and she sees herself as superior to the male with whom she has been involved. She has had the advantage of psychotherapy since her mid-adolescence, of the kind we have described: she has been free to see the therapist when *she* feels the need, as frequently or infrequently, for as short or long a duration as she herself determines.

Both the patient and her young lover, 19-year-olds, come from broken homes and have had difficulty finding a "place" for themselves with their parents' new marriages and new families. Hence they have clung to each other, excluding much of the rest of the human world. Denise was quite aware from the beginning that Bill was not as bright as she. He had dropped out of high school and had no aspirations for further education, while she was, albeit ambivalently, planning college, and already taking some courses. Since she was working and he had no job, she found herself supporting him. For some while she fought off a secret boredom, which she especially felt because of Bill's lack of insight into himself. When sex too began to pall, she told him that she wanted to "see other guys" and that he should "see other girls." He rather agreed, and set the plan in motion by moving out, and beginning to date.

But then Denise was overcome with anguish, and at this phase renewed her therapy, feeling an inner vacuum, lost and directionless. She requested frequent sessions, saying, "I want to see you to keep from calling him." She was experiencing jealousy at the thought of his being with other girls, especially of his taking them to bed. She found herself with no real desire to be with other males, and to those she did permit herself to see she denied sex. The therapist noted Denise's determination "to do something with herself," her sense that, unless she could feel stronger inside, she might simply transfer her clinging to another man. She has been able to elaborate on the value of a phase of self-repair, and has reflected sadly that Bill's not doing likewise may increase the gap that divides them. She wants him to engage in treatment too, but he shows no inclination to do so.

During this mourning period Denise had a dream of rebirth: She is falling downstairs from an enclosure, but there is a gap between the lower step and the ground. However, she falls softly to the ground and begins to crawl. Thus, we might guess that, although it has felt dangerous to make an exit from the womb of that relationship, it has not been as bad as she feared, and there are hopes of a *new beginning.*

What we observe emerging as we view the differences between these two cases is a trend toward greater toleration of tentative togetherness when a relationship cannot promise relative equality, and greater toleration of aloneness when the individual senses the need for self-repair. Denise manifested a lesser urgency to marry than did Mr. N. and a lesser urgency to leap to new relationships to cure the grief of parting. She could bear a phase of no connectedness with a lover because she saw that phase apart as prerequisite to a better interrelating. It is our view that the mode of therapy in which she has experienced no need of the therapist to hang onto her when she "felt like quitting" has afforded her both a model for parting and a confidence in her own ability to make constructive use of a period of self-retreat. This clinical approach thus emphasizes the reparative intent hidden in every symptom and complaint, even in the furies and depressions accompanying separation and divorce.

Chapter VIII

A Dialectical Spiral of Autonomy and Intimacy

There are two biblical accounts of human creation, offering alternative views of the relationship between woman and man. The first image presents two separate, equally bestowed and independent sexes, each containing the potential for omnipotence and self-sufficiency:

> So God created man in his *own* image, in the image of God created he him; male and female created he them.
>
> *Genesis, I*

The second vision describes a tender care and concern for the lowly and lonely male in need of female help to achieve wholeness and autonomy from the source:

> And the Lord God formed man of the dust of the ground, and breathed into his nostrils the breath of life, and man became a living soul.
>
> And the Lord God said, it is not good that the man should be alone. I will make him an help meet for him.
>
> And the Lord God caused a deep sleep to fall upon Adam, and he slept; and he took one of his ribs, and closed up the flesh instead thereof; And the rib which the Lord God had taken from man, made he a woman, and brought her unto the man.
>
> And Adam said, this is now bone of my bones, and flesh of my flesh; she shall be called Woman, because she was taken out of man.

> Therefore shall a man leave his father and his mother, and shall cleave unto his wife; and they shall be one flesh.
>
> *Genesis, II*

Bridging the two views, we see a pattern for both human evolution and personal development, each oscillating between a necessary connectedness and an inevitable separateness. The pace and style of oscillation and the transitions between these two axes will vary for each person and map his particular life history, his individual spiral of growth.

We have favored the thesis that a clinical therapy centered in transference analysis is the most penetrating humanistic approach into the depths and transformations of experience. Research in genetics and in neural energy processes may eventually sharpen our images of these proceedings and so improve our perspectives and increase our alternatives. Yet the beginning moments of awakening of a self, in primary illusion, may remain unclear as in a dream and the absolute fulfillment of that first promise may remain incomplete. However it is possible to describe the process and the pattern of evolution as a dialectical spiral or helix which interweaves the two dimensions of development, intimacy and autonomy, or, more academically, object-relations and narcissism. One is also tempted to speculate about cosmic models and spirits through an analogy to the nuclear physicists' unveiling of the energy processes, fusion and fission; but for now, there are complexities enough in the smaller private realms of human loving and individuation.

From Primary Illusion to Adult Mutuality

Our central hypothesis has been that the infant, in first occasions of primary gratification, glimpses a global state of paradise, free of pain or strain; he samples a blissfulness in both his elemental feeling of self and his primordial sense of home. We have identified his perception as a primary illusion, a mental representation which generalizes the qualities of flowing ease and harmony into an idealized image of existence. There is no felt need for effort or apprehension, for measure or control, about any inner or outer forces. The baby experiences these timeless and structureless qualities in a spirit of "here and now" sensuousness and a "let it all hang out" sensuality.

The working assumption basic to our clinical approach is that this primary vision imprints a model of perfect fulfillment which can guide the call for help. In a treatment atmosphere of safety as we have described it, patients spontaneously discover in themselves positive feeling tones echoing the general tenor of that illusion, and as transference analysis liberates their expressiveness, they can verbalize the benign aspects they experience. Such awareness permits a lessening of urgencies about immediate problems and a renewing of efforts to re-examine and repair longstanding feelings of burden, damage and obstruction. Their larger goal becomes that of readying themselves for a way of life closer in quality to that primary psychic state. The adult edition is seen as comprising a set of enriched processes of identification, participation and communication, all increasing the texture of mutuality while strengthening the capacities for flexible and playful autonomy.

While our clinical approach remains rooted in Freud's only absolute criterion for psychoanalysis (1914), the principle of transference analysis, certain modifications in both theory and method have been made and have been illustrated in the cases reported. A more careful redefinition of personal privacy and of the rights of self-determination, for patient and therapist, has, for us, revised details of psychotherapeutic interaction; and working these new ways has yielded us cues to a rethinking of our theories about the nature of sexual differences, their causes and their possibilities for change. The clinical process permits us to recognize in our women and men clients an inherent capacity and wish to transcend early differences with their special advantages and burdens, and to reach for a fuller yet flexible sharing of both realities and phantasies. We see such self-directed progress as a spiral of human evolution which oscillates dialectically between phases of self-repair and of rearranging the interplay of human relating; and sociologically current trends in sexual liberation and humanistic growth movements may also be understood in this light.

The infant, after early glimpses of absolute happiness, in the primary illusion, suffers inevitable falls from grace. Biological forces and surrounding resources cannot match perfectly. The best of mothers will fail her baby at times. Consequently, each child is propelled into developing its own functioning and reshaping its connections with the environment of people and things. Both constitutional forces and maturational schedules may be pre-set, in ways yet to be specified by genetics; these givens act as pressures and provisions which qualify the management of tensions and opportunities by the emerging self. Buffeted and coddled, from within and without, the person develops his own supplies, skills and connections but also is compromised by past and current experiences of faulty stores, oppression and rejection.

These unfortunate events are the raw materials for those phantasy elaborations which fester into symptoms and sufferings. The classical clinical challenge has been seen as the unravelling of the contorted and distorting phantasms in order to make conscious and clear the "fragment of lost experience" (Freud, 1937a) which instigated the malignant images and convictions torturing the patient. We have added, centrally, a reminder of the equally crucial fragment of lost benign experience, the primary illusion, which instigates the reparative processes. That combined deposit of historical truths, benign and malignant, is rediscovered as active emotional forces in the spontaneous transference projections which are liberated and revised by a clinical approach ready to allow and later interpret those regressions. This powerful deposit of psychological stalemates can convert pain to promise, hurting to hoping and new efforts.

A spiral of developmental stages etches and scratches a life history for each of us, with a unique sequence of good and bad moments and phases, and with their particular consequences of expanding pleasures and painful damages. When the primary illusion fails, a repair of the presumed perfection is demanded and required. New capacities and skills are acquired to bridge the basic faults, damaged trusting and self-doubt. We have termed the new equipments: *identifications, participations* and *communications;* and the failures are called: *deprivations, suppressions* and *frustrations.* Metapsychological theoreticians among our colleagues have established other languages for the patterns and problems in personality growth: ego structures and object-relations, defense mechanisms and character traits, and those official categories of neuroses, psychoses and elusive borderlines.

We believe that our words describing qualities of experience are closer to felt meanings of basic self-expression and so may be more useful in recognizing and describing the patient's signals as he reaches, unconsciously, through his misshapen forms of ambivalent hopes and dreads, for a glimpse of the original bliss. These reachings, verbal and non-verbal, constitute the transference regressions which are the challenge for analytic therapy. We have illustrated ways by which the strains of edgy battling and of defeating stalemate can be converted into a working alliance. Each occasion of a liberating transference interpretation frees another piece of repaired autonomy and renews hope for intimacy with a mutually selected other.

The therapist, like the good enough mother, must be flexibly responsive while remaining a private person and not vulnerable to the patient's projections of positive and negative feelings. This relationship can have real caring and moments of sharing offered from both sides, but not in whole-hearted equal intimacy. The illusion of mutuality is part of the patient's process of self-repair; the reliving with the therapist of the emotional conflict is a self-provoked risking, an unconscious reaching for a better autonomy. The therapist is consciously intent on liberating the patient from feeling the need to expend himself in clinging or in combatting, or in any other defensive manner of wasting his goods. In these unequal conditions there is no even exchange possible, but a felt deprivation or suppression. The medium of change is the process of dissolving of the patient's deeply ambivalent primary involvement by a gentle acceptance and then interpretation of the whole spontaneous transference, both sides of the regression, the magical and the monstrous, the benign and the malignant qualities in the secondary defensive illusions or phantasies. The glimpses of positive primary illusion with the analyst works to restore the courage and capacity to create anew that illusion, so essential to whole-hearted loving, now with more playfulness and with a flexibility to find more equal circumstances than in therapy.

The Path of Self-Reparative Regression

Benign illusions with the therapist can free the patient to leave feeling ready to engage in a more complete edition of flexible sharing, of intimacy balanced by autonomy, with a more mutually selected partner. The development of such elasticity and adaptability is never absolute but the patient gains resiliency and buoyancy by knowing his vulnerabilities to unconscious repetitions of significant failures. Equipped with self-insight, the person can transform the compelling power of old wishes and fears into a reparation, through a regression, a renewing return, and a new beginning.

When Freud's first patient dared to reprimand her Doctor and demand his tolerant and non-intrusive attention (see Chapter III), she might have been given a severe reproof or an unfriendly dismissal. By insisting on respect for her pace and measure of tensions, she risked a further trauma. The fortunate outcome of her potentially provocative behavior was advantageous for her, and for the further development of a theory and method of psychotherapy. Bold complaining may be a path to recovering the spontaneity of earlier wishes which have been festering into binding symptoms anchored in unconscious ambivalence.

Some of us have been working with "experienced patients," who have had many years of psychotherapy with perhaps a series of therapists of various types and schools. Such insistent clients are often diagnosed, and abandoned, as narcissistic characters with severe pathologies, too difficult or too clever, even too psychopathic for established methods and theories. Freud reported his own failures to engage such patients into a workable transference process. But there are recent efforts (e.g., Kohut, 1971 and 1977, and Kernberg, 1975) to meet the special challenge of these more self-centered persons. In these efforts there is an acceptance of the possible value of some regressive periods without the orthodox insistence on or immediate exposure and interpretation of the defensive aggressiveness in the patient's seeming refusal to cooperate. There is a new leeway for the expression of more primitive and unrealistic demandingness, especially by sophisticated patients who may have some notion of the reparative possibilities of open, free-associative complaining.

We are proposing that narcissistic regression is necessary and inherent to the advance of skills and resources for better exchanges, better relating, better sharing. In several previous chapters, we have shown our debt to the writings of Darwin

(1871), Ferenczi (1929), Winnicott (1971), and Balint (1969) for groundwork in this direction. Now we add our own refinements of perspective and our clinical approach.

We have stressed the dialectic nature of human development with its phases of thesis, antithesis and then a new synthesis. The emergence of adult intimacy has been described as a product of two persistent dimensions of intense search: first, the effort to formulate one's individual identity, and second, having formed it, the risk to suspend concern with oneself while focussing on the qualities of a potential mate. When a right matching is felt, a crisis occurs within, because the highly valued identity may be lost in the merging being sought. How often has literature described the dilemma; the hero or heroine "falls" in love and feels beside himself or herself when love is tendered. The traumatic step has been safely made when the loving is reciprocated in mutualities and a new synthesis is made. Each deepening of the union entails another bit of crisis and a trauma is risked and overcome.

This romantic image is a highlighting, we suggest, of the essential dialectic necessary at all turnings and transitions of every close relationship. Complications are increased when the sense of identity is not well formed but remains significantly undeveloped and unconscious. Then one's perceptions of the other can hardly be clear and objective; one's hidden needs project images of both phantastic dangers and impossible fulfillments. The crisis here becomes a severe trauma; the person has suffered additional evidence of narcissistic inadequacy and the hope for reparation has failed. The serious crisis has made more complex any fresh move for better autonomy or intimacy. Restoration, restitution, repair becomes necessary.

Reparation is part of the aim of all creative activity including the private narcissistic aspects of play and illusions (Shor, 1953). When "object relations" fail, the reparative aim may include efforts to repair oneself, as well as the repairing of bad or destroyed objects. "Character neuroses" are especially likely to contain damaged body ego functions; these weaknesses may be bound up with layers of never verbalized dread about lasting damage to one's functions of instinctual expression. Here, too, analysis may facilitate a process of self-provocation in the patient, so that he evokes in himself more of these anxieties obstructing his possession and use of deeper narcissistic resources. Then analysis makes possible new function pleasures and a closer sharing with confirming others. The person becomes selective.

Children, in the hope of externalizing "bad objects," often provoke their parents to manifest hostile attitudes, to show their hand. The child may thus achieve a clearer perspective for making further ego defenses, if not too traumatized (Coleman and Shor, 1953). During analysis as adult patients, they come to learn how such provocations emerge from their unconscious dreads about their parent's unconscious attitudes. The provocative incidents are reported as occurring between the ages of six and twelve years and are persistently recalled during treatment as justification for character weaknesses. These "screen memories" are repeated and similar provocations are expressed in the transference until the provocative aim is interpreted. Thus analysis permits the patient to recall and reconstruct the reparative aims concealed behind the longstanding screen memories of these crucial traumatic events. We come to understand how the exposure of parental hostility recurrently resulted in fresh trauma too severe to allow the child then to recognize consciously his wish to repair the parent. The self-traumatization backfired, until transference analysis confirmed the wish to test for fuller relating, for possible change and repair.

Our clinical emphasis on providing the safe play atmosphere to free the expression and exploration of narcissistic illusions avoids the accumulation of additional trauma. And it permits an awareness of constructive learning from a deliberate daring to provoke oneself and others.

Self-provocation is an experiment, a testing of inner reality, the forces in oneself. When the provocation fails to allow a working through to a better position for ego defense, the attempt has usually been called a "repetition compulsion" or a "masochistic acting-out"; both terms have been identified as expressions of Freud's *Death Instinct.* A successful self-provocation will lead to the relinquishing of a damaged sense of self, and the establishing of a stronger narcissistic phase, in preparation for a better pattern of object relationship. In this sense, a successful self-provocation is a constructive acting-out.

The consciously self-directed acting-out may yield a discharge of anxiety about an instinctual component and allow the patient to make a clearer measure of his pain and pleasure, and their origins. Such knowledge equips the ego for a more precise management of its sources and resources, and fosters the spiral interweaving creative and flexible ego development with relating to others. The regression has become reparative.

Several of our case studies have illustrated fresh problems which are disrupting and confusing the patients who are pioneering in sexual liberation. When they ask for "complete honesty" to one another, they soon feel a need to keep some privacy, especially about unresolved inner problems. They then ask for more implicit trusting, instead of compulsive confessions. When they offer each other sexual freedom, there is some uneasiness about what violates faithfulness; and they suffer shame about feeling jealous or possessive or revengeful. The complaints are made in a spirit of surprise and embarrassment rather than horror, fury or flight. Less terrified than in the past, they become curious to unearth the persisting or recurring anxieties evoked in living out the images of innocence and spontaneity which are implicit to the primary illusion.

The promising clinical discovery is that there is more tolerance for expressing primitive wishes and anxious phantasies which seem to the patients to be profoundly irrational and unrealizable. They bear with free associations about paranoid sensitivities in themselves and in their intimates: states of overwhelming vulnerability to attacking forces, to raging greed and impulses of destructive envy, even sensations of fragmentation of their sense of being a self. They recognize in their depressions a need to protect themselves from the loss of all privacy and autonomy; through a process of constructive mourning they suspend their dread of abandonment to allow a narcissistic phase of repairing their own suppressed and damaged capacities to feel more at home in themselves. This reduced desperation about inner disorder becomes more possible because they also glimpse the timeless pleasures of benign regression in the safe clinical setting; these positive occasions are followed by a less urgent attention to the therapist's reviews and interpretations of the evident course of their primary wishes, disruptive anxieties and defensive compromises. Such patterns are illustrated from the shared transference observations and supported by reference to specific life history data.

It is our belief that a fuller working-through of these paranoid and depressive anxieties is more possible in individual analytic psychotherapy than in the popular group procedures and other approaches where careful, detailed transference observation and interpretation is not possible, not welcomed, and sometimes even high-handedly ridiculed. When society permits more glimpses of the primary illusion, there erupts an impatience for perfect instant intimacy, and even trained psychotherapists leap to dispense quick-sell methods and theories to an eager clientele.

Celebration in Mutual Regression

Our view is that there is a special value of individual psychoanalytic psychotherapy for the rediscovery of the qualities of primary illusion and for the recovery of capacities to protect and enjoy such regression in adult life. This personal and professional perspective is derived from the original maternal model of supplying and sheltering the budding self so carefully that it can safely and self-selectively play and explore at its own pace while it learns its current resources and limitations. In therapy too, the emerging person becomes equipped to decide to leave, ready for a larger autonomy and a deeper relating. Having internalized the model, the individual can advance from the uneven professional relationship, to seek more equal exchange where more profound risking in more complete regressions is possible. This dialectic of making progressive gains in order to protect and supply regressive gratifications is the philosophical premise imbedded in our clinical approach. We shall review the speculative cues to this pattern in realms beyond individual development in the appended postlude; here we propose a more detailed demonstration of the essential model in the context of loving intimacy, substantiated directly by clinical data with our most "progressed" patients.

This clinical perspective is revolutionary, we feel, for orthodox psychoanalytic theory and method. Classical formulations have emphasized the goal of public responsibility and rationality; Freud centrally promised, "Where Id was, there shall Ego be" (1923). His invocation of Eros, with its ever-expanding connecting, was welcomed widely, but he was branded pessimistic when he gave equal consideration to Thanatos, a principle of simplification of psychic bindings and other organic structures (1920). He speculated about this dualism and finally came to warn (1938) that the traditional emphasis on self-integration and ego synthesis was "clearly at fault." Nonetheless the one-sided value-preference for realistic maturity has remained dominant with few exceptions. Kris relieved somewhat the high-minded severity by his formulation, "Regression in the service of the ego" (1952). And, in the last decade, a few analysts have allowed and utilized regressive phases in the treatment of specially difficult character disorders (e.g., Kohut, 1971). We have been describing a clinical approach which recognizes regressions as both inevitable and essential for fundamental reparations in all clients.

Our approach has been provoked and nourished by Balint's highly original conception, "Progression for the Sake of Regression" (1959). When the pervading aim is a benign unstructuring of the self, then individual development and human evolution can be freer of pre-determined directions and pre-set stages. Our reports of spontaneous reaching for play and illusion, when the patient feels safe enough, support the new emphasis; this valuing of the illusion of absolute innocence is especially evident in emerging attitudes and experiments in male-female relationships. In order to play well, our patients accept the task of preparing themselves with an effective awareness of inner and outer resources and pitfalls; such progress can protect all regressive experiences, from the simplest play to the deepest intimacy. All forms of art, work and loving can contain components of the primary illusion. The inter-play of genital love may be the most extreme, the most complete expression; it can emerge from and develop with the matured resources for physiological and psychological experiencing within each of the partners.

The experience of perfect mature sexual intercourse can be understood as a stage, a phase of the life cycle with the richest mutual regression, made possible by preparatory progression in the lovers, both separately and together. In their act of intimacy, they will move through unifying communication, participation and finally into complete identification, potentially leading to a cosmic celebration in mutual orgasm. It is a constructive victory of illusion over concrete, proven reality. The sexual elaboration of the model can demonstrate how a joint regression in genital loving permits a renewal of individuality and prevents a deposit of paranoid or depressive reactions in each of the partners.

Freud comments, in *Beyond the Pleasure Principle* (1920):

> We have all experienced how the greatest pleasure attainable by us, that of the sexual act, is associated with a momentary extinction of a highly intensified excitation. The binding of an instinctual impulse would be a preliminary function designed to prepare the excitation for its final elimination in the pleasure of discharge.

Human coitus entails the effort to combine two ego aims: the managing of a mounting excitement of psychic sensitivity, in foreplay, and the risking of a profound psychic extinction, in discharge. Failure maintains an intensified anxiety-tension state. Success signals a mastery, by a balancing of ego tolerance for excitement with ego flexibility for extinction. The achievement of genital sex is the effective balancing of larger burdens of libidinal tension (Eros) with risks of masochistic extinction (Thanatos). The resultant discharge in orgasm is crucial for the economy of the entire psyche.

Ferenczi's dictum suggests a dramatic perspective for this experience of total victory (1926):

> By its very nature intercourse should not be a deliberate act, a matter of use and wont, but a sort of celebration, during which dammed-up energies can spend themselves in an archaic fashion.

Foreplay is the heightening of the level of narcissistic ego-expansion: the sense of vitality and abundance of psychic bindings, as well as the sense of aliveness, or erectility, of the body ego. Consequently, rich verbal and non-verbal contact is desired, a genuine "sharing" and significant stimulation of one another's crucial interests. Each is ready for a note of fresh mutual discovery, a new quality of personal contact, a transcending of previous identity. A spontaneous meeting emerges. Techniques of sexual stimulation may contribute bio-vegetatively to ego aliveness when sought and accepted as an expression of welcome and of willingness to participate, to give and take. The play, at first fun, then feels significant, serious, crucial. The spirit of joint greeting transcends, for each, any fetishistic fixations, any partial, split-off components, any private urgency or desperate need.

The penis is invited and feels invited; it rises to the occasion. The pre-coital fluids run to meet and facilitate entry and the penis can sense the vaginal walls embracing it in a warm greeting. With each gentle exploratory thrust, the penis seeks a confirmation of its aliveness and "power" in the adaptive enveloping by the vagina. The vagina responds with a reaching forward to fully stroke and stimulate itself against the firm but adaptive penis position; the woman also can seek confirmation of her inner aliveness by a friendly exploitation of the friendly phallus. Each partner engages in alternating introjection and projection, "in mutual compensation" (Ferenczi), verified in the immediate realities of one another's responsiveness, moment to moment. The joint action fosters a gathering together, a readying of the psychic load for discharge.

This process of oscillation evolves into a rich rhythm of mutual and coordinated confirmation of one another. They are now together forever, and each separation calls for a renewal of the sense of eternal connection. The "danger" in the primary love-object disappears and the ego feels freer to yield to the sense of complete regression. The contacts quicken, allowing the complete concentration of consciousness upon the sense of togetherness, until the conscious boundaries of self are extended and diffused into the primary unity. The full yielding to the instinctual flood is preceded by a final phase, a moment of forceful affirmation, of absolute assertion of oneself. Then the climax, the intense energy discharge in deep neuro-muscular contractions in the pelvis, for each of the partners.

End-pleasure radiates in the glowing narcissistic recovery from the drastic overwhelming to which the ego has subjected itself. That moment of extinction of any consciousness of self was a triumph over the dread of absolute psychic destruction. There is further reassurance in the easy renewal and revival of the sense of acceptance and love, now in quieter touching, in stillness, in spontaneous mutual gratefulness to one another, in a two-way tenderness. The primary illusion was re-experienced, enriched in an adult edition.

The partners will each regain ego control and balance, in a new psychic and physiologic economy, free of a large burden of neural tensions. They may now separate as joint victors, in peace, knowing that their coitus was an event, occurring between them and through the medium of their particular physiological structures and psychic bindings, their mutual awarenesses of body and self. It was not an act of conquest by one over the other, but a celebration of two becoming one, to the limits of physical realities and psychological identities (Shor, 1954).

We may question the degree of identicality possible in the experiences of male and female orgasm, in view of the differing physiology, different body egos. Female structure allows potentially a more diffuse, reverberating response and discharge; man's structure facilitates a briefer but pointed intensity. Yet, there are trends toward a transcending rapprochement.

Women patients now openly assert their "horniness" and general sexual aggressiveness, sometimes claiming a phase of autonomous orgasms either by masturbation or by exploitation of an available male. In response, men are increasingly accepting phases of impotence or withdrawing from sexual encounters, using the period for reviewing old anxieties and guilts, and perhaps to discover that ejaculation, per se, is a short-circuiting of a more complete psychic and body experience. There are evidences that they are coming to envy women their pervasive orgasm experience, possibly as a new manifestation of an archaic womb-envy. Each explores the other's ways, thus extending the range and depth of inner aliveness and enhancing empathy with each other. They come closer to the primary illusion.

The ultimate forms of adult mutuality are not predictable or even definable. What is most profoundly valued and enjoyed is the *process* of transcending any sense of unchosen difference or of distance, thus feeling a flowing toward undifferentiated, unstructured unity. Separate individuality is yielded to unordered intimacy, a kind of benign chaos.

We can never achieve the permanently peaceful paradise; nor can we give up the regressive wishes for it. Thus, no state of happiness will prevent forever the resurgence of further evolution. Even Kinsey's research (1953), using gross concepts and in crude ways, concludes: "Interestingly enough, this improvement in the quality of coitus in marriage had occurred coincidentally with some reduction in the frequencies of marital coitus in the course of the four decades covered by the available sample." The experience of fusion can free the person from fixation to any specific expression, even though it was previously chosen, welcomed and found deeply gratifying. Neither known pleasure nor hard reality will prevent the renewal of that ultimate aim of primary illusion. Neither fusion nor autonomy can be a lasting resting place. The ongoing interplay between these two lines of development seems always to need further healing, further movement along both dimensions—the double helix grows on.

The next curve of the spiral may extend the state of benign chaos to realms beyond the known forms of individuality and intimacy. Social change can enlarge the human playground and make it safe for more players to risk suspending old personal and group identities. Energies are freed to explore wider connections and form more flexible identities. That richer empathy will have its turn in human evolution.

Postlude: Toward the Enjoyment of Benign Chaos

We have taken the position that every individual life manifests a dialectic approach toward the re-creation of the primary illusion in loving and being, combining intimacy and individuality. A double spiral weaves the shape and texture of the personal experiencing of one's biological and social energies and forces. Analogous processes may exist in realms beyond psychology, from group living to cosmic forces. The same unconscious aims may motivate the inclination of societies to oscillate between phases emphasizing individual freedoms and phases restricting liberties for the welfare of the community. Anthropologists describe alternating Apollonian and Dionysian values in cultures: periods stressing rational control and periods stressing emotional discharging, or valuing instrumentality and then valuing expressiveness. In physiology we learn of anabolic and catabolic functions; Freud borrowed this contrast for his dualism of Eros and Thanatos, the expansive and the simplifying principles. Geneticists have offered the model of the double helix to delineate the workings of chromosomal reproduction and differentiation in evolution. Nuclear physicists now derive energy from two contrary forms of explosion, fission and fusion. Throughout nature there seem to be dialectical spirals, bringing unity out of diversity, and releasing a new diversity out of that new unity, and so forth, ad infinitum.

We are tempted to speculate about cosmic forces, but perhaps it is enough challenge to project our thesis onto the turns and twists of social evolution. We would like to play with some afterthoughts about new freedoms in a society in which a substantial number of people consciously pursue creative illusions. Can we anticipate changes in personal and social attitudes if our dialectic model is extrapolated to current conflicts within and between cultures?

Rising Expectations

Since the 1940's, there has been a series of crises and catastrophes both nationally and internationally. From this disorder and chaos, peoples have brought forth revised identities and modified their priorities and methods. They have revolted, and regrouped, shifting power balances and upsetting forever former hierarchical arrangements between haves and have-nots. The Roosevelt-Churchill pronouncements of the Four Freedoms, during World War II, had evoked a spirit of rising expectations for much of humankind: *freedom from want, from fear, freedom of speech* and *of worship.*

Many of the Western nations progressed substantially toward these liberties, achieving their abundances at increasing cost to non-technological areas of the world. The less developed peoples began to protest loudly that they felt deprived, suppressed and frustrated. These complaints were heard and elicited more empathy than ever before (Sanville, J. and Shor, J., 1975b). The international tensions reverberated in class conflicts and in private consciences. An array of reactions became manifest, from the relinquishing of longstanding imperialistic exploitations to the hardening of secret, subverting totalitarian oppressions at home and abroad. Social welfare systems developed in highly capitalistic countries as a sharing of private and state abundances. Many individuals and organized groups began to rebuff and renounce the compulsive pursuit of progress, the old achievement orientation, the traditionally prescribed social roles. A central conflict developed, between, on the one hand, a surging demand for fuller and richer private life experience, and, on the other, a wish for wider sharing and a diminution of feelings of alienation.

This dialectic is producing fresh messages and measures of priorities and pleasures, beyond those derived from unconscious dreads of infinite scarcity. As people abandon old obsessions with material supplies and powers, they can come to play at social roles, aware that they are playing, their identities acquiring a resilience and flexibility heretofore unknown in adult life. There are many indications of reflective redefinitions of goals, personal and social, in a variety of secular and spiritual concerns; for example, about ecology, population control, medium technology, energy conservation, detente and ecumenism. Simultaneous with these retreats from maximum exploitativeness, there is a proliferation of educational and training resources for self-improvement and more sensitive relating, for both narcissism and connectedness.

Four Further Freedoms

In an emerging spirit of vitality and creativity, rooted in a brave, sometimes brash, confidence and innocence, some daring spirits display, some publicly and some privately, a next phase beyond the search for abundance. The new ideal is for a more flowing pace of being and relating. It values more experiences of flexible exchange and sharing of feelings and meanings with others who are accepted as equal and offer valued differences. These new individual and social attitudes and interests are expressible in a set of four further freedoms; they are expressions of play, of benign illusion in living:

Freedom to Want—and to reflect on alternatives (e.g., to search, to know, to know how, to feel and to do for one's own wishes and hopes)

To want more "fulfillment" of one's undeveloped potentialities.

To want more mutuality through greater equality in personal relationships.

To want more participation in "political-social" decisions to effect change in one's total way of life.

Freedom to Fear—and to explore long-hidden exaggerated aspects of terror (e.g., to make one's own measures of dangers to body, mind and spirit)

To fear being shaped into fixed roles demanding denial of aspects of self.

To fear being pressured by personal needs of anxious others into rigid role-playing relationships.

To fear being forced by social-political powers to submit to "popular" persuasion as for status, prestige, or against isolation.

Freedom Not to Speak—and yet to protect privacies and personal choices (e.g., to feel safe to explore one's inner thoughts and feelings)

Free to withdraw to privacy and "repair" oneself.

Free to enjoy silent companionship.

Free to delay and refrain from public commitments.

Freedom Not to Believe—but to feel the courage of not knowing and not believing old answers (e.g., to revise traditions, review old dogma, and even accept not understanding)

Free to question any "authority" claiming final answers about personal values.

Free to explore and experiment with the processes of enriching personal relationships, free of public pressure.

Free to rethink the basic social and political philosophies and processes effecting us all.

These further freedoms will supplement the original four as we increase our tolerance and attention to the messages and meanings being fashioned at the frontiers of society. We are listening to the sounds and flurries of many newly vocal "minorities": sexual, ethnic, occupational, age-grouped, geographical, handicapped, exceptional, and more. The obstacles to harmony are more sharply identified in these periods of noisy contention, all as phases of antithesis necessary to the larger dialectic evolution. The psychic unity of mankind now encourages our empathy and implements it as well; the potentials for closer identification, participation and communication become more actual.

We recognize a possible note of Pollyana and panacea in the spirit of our approach: its promising of new beginnings. It is an optimistic thesis, favoring play, self-expression, self-pacing, reparative intention and primary illusion. A hint of naivete might be attributed to a perspective which seems to encourage and value feelings of irresponsible innocence and risky spontaneity. There is an element of truth in these charges; yet we know that self-awareness about such regressions and about their specific vulnerabilities is a protection for a possible liberation. Pathology and malignancy can be avoided or diminished.

We do wish to re-affirm our belief in the clinical principle that benign regression can liberate energies and efforts for the further evolution of human intimacy and individuality. We acknowledge the special protections with which we surround our patients but we also observe that changing morality and laws provide increasing safety at large for exploration and experimentation, for trial and error. As liberation movements and personal self-discovery reinforce each other, people work to re-form their public and private expressions of individuality and connectedness. The progress which makes possible the fuller regression to moments of experiencing primary illusion occurs on three levels: greater abundance of supplies for individually felt and individually measured needs; increasing freedom to express oneself in safe spontaneity; fuller sharing of meanings and feelings with self-selected and valued others.

Psychoanalysis can play its part as a catalyst at the frontiers of consciousness, naturally and properly at the margin of conventional respectability to do its special work. Although only a small self-selective sample of people may choose to use this method, we guess that they are among those whose drive for primary love is the stronger and yet more harnessed to an equally powerful urge for that autonomy which can protect the illusion of fusion. The insights they gain are continuously diffused into social awareness through all the media of modern communication (Kris, E., Herma, H. and Shor, J., 1943).

Social evolution works to develop new persons and some reach for professional help to explore their next edges of uncertainty. Open therapists will suspend their own certainties and listen and look to fresh forms of complaint and aspiration. Psychoanalytic method is a catalyst for further evolution and yet it will itself be modified as experienced patients challenge the professional therapist with deeper demands for more reparative regressions. The baseline of benign chaos in the primary illusion favors the development of richer editions of adult love, work and play.

Freud's advice for the good life, that one aim to achieve satisfaction from love and work, may now be expanded. We speak for including the qualities of playfulness and for allowing them to permeate living. Thus we hope to reach the love in work and in play; to enjoy the work in love and in play; and, most deeply, to explore the play in working and in loving.

Appendix A:

Rethinking Female-Male Development

by Jean Sanville

Paper presented as the Norma Wandesforde Memorial Lecture, University of Washington, February, 1976.

In her provocative book, *The Descent of Woman*, Elaine Morgan begins by pointing out how much of the thinking of evolutionists has been androcentric (male centered), and that this habit of thinking has caused scientists not only to overlook valuable clues to our ancestry but has led them "into making statements that are errant and demonstrable nonsense." She suggests that it is time to approach the whole thing again right from the beginning: "this time from the distaff side, and along a totally different route." Her imaginative reconstruction of evolutionary theory from the point of view of the female leads to fresh concepts about the origins of humankind, to a different view of the present, and to exciting speculations about the future.

Today's women, in their search for liberation from roles of subordination and inferiority, are inciting clinicians to rethink their theories about the psychosexual development of women, their concepts of female psychology, and in short, to rid themselves of those androcentric habits of thinking which have led them into erratic and foolish notions about the feminine psyche. Both as theoreticians and as therapists, we must plead guilty to their legitimate complaints that we have been prejudicial in our attitudes and that, in our clinical interventions, we have all too often aimed at the adjustment of woman to her biologically and culturally assigned roles of wife and mother. If we are willing to reconsider our traditional positions, to open ourselves to new data, we may arrive at greatly improved theories of human growth and development altogether and at superior clinical procedures for working with clients of both sexes who are seeking to disentangle themselves from the constricting functions and roles which have prevailed until recently. We may attain an expanded sense of the individual potential for both men and women, and of their conjoint potential for richer relationships.

It may well be women who will come to the rescue of our science, for they are demanding to be heard and seen afresh, and to the rescue of our art, for they ask nothing less than that psychotherapy help to free them from both biology and culture.

New knowledge is coming from biological researches inspired by a fresh zeal to comprehend the nature of sex differences, from close longitudinal studies on infancy and mothering, and from recent perceptions of sensitive clinicians. It is of significance that much of the new data has been unearthed by women: Sibylle Escalona and Mary Leitch with their studies of innate differences in infants (1949 and 1953), Sibylle Escalona with her further research into the roots of individuality (1968), Margaret Mahler with her observations of separation-individuation (1975), Eleanor Galenson with her studies on early genitality (1972), Phyllis Greenacre with her speculations on the state of infancy (1971), Berta Bornstein with her clinical reports including the continuation of masturbation in latency (1951), and Judith Kestenberg with her keen descriptions of the differences in body movements of mothers with girl and with boy babies (1975). For the most imaginative picture of the earliest period of human life we are indebted to Melanie Klein and her school. Many of her ideas, especially about the origins of envy in childhood (1957), are potentially most fruitful for our considerations.

And so, let us try to rewrite individual psychosexual development with an emphasis on the distaff side, noting certain advantages enjoyed by the female, so that we may try to understand why males seem to be lagging in breaking away from old roles and why they so often avoid or flee from clinical help. We will permit ourselves some playful extrapolations on current knowledge gleaned from these diverse sources. The story might then read as follows:

In the beginning mother nature first creates woman. Every human fetus begins life as female, and in about half of all pregnancies the fetus continues its unfolding of those bodily traits natural to the female of the species. In the other half, however, a foreign substance called an androgen enters the picture and its effect is to suppress some of the embryo's tendency toward femininity and to substitute that morphology and physiology which we call masculine. Rather than as Freud pronounced, "the little girl is a little man," (1931), we might now say, "the little boy is a little woman."

The infant's discovery of its bodily shape and contours occurs much earlier than we once thought. Both girl and boy babies discover their genitals in the first weeks of life, and their fondling of them is an important aspect of the beginning of body ego, a forerunner of identity as male or female. That is, this happens if there is a mother who feeds and holds and touches tenderly. Harlow's monkey babies, reared by cloth mothers, did not discover their genitality, and even by several years of age could not learn to copulate. Spitz' institutional babies did not masturbate, but instead engaged in such auto-erotic activities as head banging and rocking (1949).

Every baby lives first in a state of prenatal unity with the mother, and we speculate that in his or her early postnatal life, the infant still experiences self as at one with the mother, to the extent, that is, that its needs are promptly met and gratified. If the mother is sensitive and unanxious and enjoys her caretaking, the infant may begin to experience pleasure in those fleeting but increasingly frequent moments of selfhood. But if mother is insufficiently sensitive or emotionally unavailable, or if the child experiences serious illness, hospitalization, or surgical intervention, then a degree of instability in body outline, including genitals, ensues, with a consequent instability in the sense of self, and with a fear of fragmentation or dissolution. It is this precariousness that renders the child prone later to develop symptomatic castration reaction. We will discuss that shortly.

We note that the girl baby arrives at birth with physical characteristics like those of the mother who bore her. This circumstance would appear to facilitate the mother's identification with her, and to make her ministrations and responses different from those that she offers to a son. Among the lower primates it has been noted that in the first ninety days of her infant's life the mother who bears a female holds, restrains and fondles her more, is tender and loving, while, should she have a male baby, she cuffs him around, and even "presents to him" sexually (Mitchell, 1968). Observations on human mothers with their infants suggests that women treat girl babies as extensions of themselves and very early deal with the boy as disparate. Much clinical data which unearths deeply subjective reactions confirms that unconsciously the little daughter is regarded as "part of me," while the son is experienced as "other." Two mothers currently in treatment, each with a son and a daughter, have both struggled with their more profound identification with the girl. Each has said, "I would be sad and grieving if something happened to him, but if she were to die, I would die."

We might surmise from this that the little girl has more occasions than does the boy of experiencing that blissful sense of primary fusion with source which becomes the prototype for all subsequent loving. She may be more accustomed to feeling invited to physical and psychological contact, and hence may be freer to reach for it herself. Thus, although Freud declared that the mother-son relationship is "altogether the most perfect, the most free of ambivalence of all human relationships" (1932), we should perhaps revise that statement.

If this line of thinking is correct, we would predict that the little girl would gather a lesser load of reactive aggression and hostility, that she would, much earlier than the boy, have available to her "more neutralized energy" which could be used for socialization. Indeed that does appear to be so. Again, among rhesus monkey babies, the males are said to be more irritable, to bite their mothers more (Mitchell, 1968). Among human infants, little girls are, for example, much more easily trained. They are pliant, not perhaps out of the "greater need for affection," as Freud thought, but out of gratitude to source for having received greater affection. Clinically, we observe few cases of encopresis, involuntary defecation, in girls.

We have no statistical evidence, but in our clinical experience we have treated more adult males than females whose beginning sense of autonomy in childhood was disrupted by mothers invading their bodies with constant enemas. Such men are often wary of the words of the female therapist, as though words too would have the power to take away what they are not ready to give. One patient, disappointed that he had, through undue frugality, missed an opportunity to buy a certain boat, which had symbolized for him both autonomy and a sort of cocoon where he would be self-sufficient, all needs gratified, dreamed that he was trying and trying to have a bowel movement but was totally constipated. He also played out, via his payments, whether the therapist would demand his check at the first of the month, that is at a time which suited her, or would permit him to delay until later, at a time when it was convenient for him.

The erection so regularly reported in the boy baby when he is frustrated in the feeding situation suggests that very early there tends to be a link between sexuality and aggression for him. Even when he is fed, we might guess that it does not necessarily result in genital pleasure in the same fashion as for the girl. For she, late into fetal life, has possessed a cloaca, a sort of combined anal and vaginal opening, and even after birth the two areas of the body are closely adjacent. When the baby girl receives a good feed, there are contractions in the anal area which are most likely virtually indistinguishable from vaginal sensations in their pleasurable aspect (Greenacre, 1971). Thus, her earliest genitality may be tied to the rudiments of love while his may be linked with primitive hostility. Perhaps here are the forerunners of his need for conquest, to take what he does not expect to be freely given.

Latent Burdens in Male Individuation

That phase which Mahler has called separation-individuation may be more drastic for the boy. Children of both sexes, equipped around the middle of the second year of life with greater mobility, make excursions away from mother. Both, however, like to have her there for their periodic return, and so she is. But perhaps traditionally she has been more likely actively to encourage the boy's goings-away and to discourage subtly his rapprochments to her. Perhaps there has tended to be the message that his place is out there in the world, and regression is not favored. Therefore, we might guess that motor behavior for the boy might easily be used in the service of defense. Some confirmation of this is that eight out of ten children diagnosed as hyperactive are boys. Traditionally too, the little girl, although finding mother pleased with her newly found independence, notes also that mother welcomes her return to the maternal presence. If we were to use the language of Michael Balint (1959) we would say that in the girl child ocnophilic, or clinging tendencies, that is, toward connectedness, have been fostered while the boy's philobatic, freely moving tendencies, that is, toward self-sufficiency, have been encouraged.

Freud's observation (1931) about the relatively long duration of the girl's attachment to the mother led him to surmise that the preoedipal period was of greater importance in female development. Today we would see it as equally important for the male, but simply setting him off on a different course. We might anticipate changes in this differentiation as mothers move to claim more of their self-sufficiency, and tend to see in the clinging child an obstacle. Hence they would consciously wish to foster independence in daughters as well as sons. Preoedipal children today, unlike in Freud's time, more often have fuller relationships with parents of both sexes, as fathers too partake of nurturant roles.

But until recently, the girl baby's possibly greater gratification from her mother may have acted to diminish the inevitable sense of disappointment in source. Moreover, the door of return has been more widely open to her, and her infantile dependency not as likely to be prematurely disrupted. May this not be one factor that makes her less inclined later on to see changing lovers as the answer to frustrations? Girls in our culture have generally made more constant relationships than have boys with both parents and peers at stages of life even prior to adult intimacy. Females seem less driven to make urgent choices or changes. When they do shift their allegiances, we can look for less desperate motives than penis envy or compensation for castration.

Freud, however, pondering why the girl would ever turn from the mother whom he saw as having been so exclusively loved, came up with the notion that the little girl resented her mother for the latter's failure to equip her with a penis, and that when the mother herself came to be seen as "castrated" she was depreciated altogether. Out of her genital disappointment, the little girl was presumed to reach for father to get what mother withheld, a compensatory motive. Today, with changes in family structure, our increasingly detailed observations of children at this stage of life reveal a progressive motive, that of separation as a necessary phase in the process of individuation. The girl must move away from the identification with and the interdependence on mother if she is to become differentiated from her and to discover that there are others in whom she can place trust. Contact with a variety of persons will give her alternate models for aspects of her own personality, and the new interactional challenges and rewards will promote the proliferation of social skills. We see a peculiar fixity and rigidity in certain types of children, such as those that present the problem of school phobia, when they have not been able successfully to negotiate that separation.

Clinically we find it essential to attend to the emotional climate of the shift from the preoccupation with mother to fascination with father. The girl must feel that her mother permits this shift and will not abandon her. We see pathological consequences when the mother can not relinquish her little girl, or when her tie to her husband is so tenuous that she perceives her daughter's turning to him as competition with her. The father on his part ideally recognizes his daughter in nonsexual ways, yet without rejecting her sexuality. Only when a "climate of revenge" between mother and father or between mother and daughter pertains do we observe the old Medea complex. There are, unfortunately, fathers who may delight in competing with their wives for the child's affection, and there are fathers inclined to be overtly seductive with their little girls.

Must we now discard the notion of penis envy? No, Freud's notion of that phenomenon, reconstructed in adult analysis, is confirmed by observational data today. As children in the second year of life discover others of the opposite sex, boys do develop castration reactions and girls do develop penis envy.

But we note several concomitants: It is an age when children generally feel greed and envy the possessions of others, and when cognitive development is such that what is not seen does not exist. At the same time there is some felt threat of object loss in the child's movements away from mother. Under "good-enough" circumstances the child leaves and return playfully, testing both inner resources and the reliability of source. As he or she becomes more confident about growing autonomy, envy of others diminishes, learning occurs about sex differences, and castration fears and penis envy are left behind, simply phase-specific anxieties.

We might now observe that the little girl does not exchange mother for father but rather adds a capacity for object love to her capacity for identification. Mother remains for her a person whom she feels herself to be like, and her father tends to foster that identification. His daughter wants to resemble the woman whom he loves, and he reinforces this by encouraging her to emulate mother. Moreover mother remains the main source of care in our society, where father is likely to be somewhat absentee, and thus perhaps more of an abstraction than a reality. We might ponder too the likelihood that in his absence he may be more idealized by children of both sexes.

For the boy also the mother remains the main source of care, but by the oedipal period, he must already repress his felt dependency needs and gratify them mainly covertly. His father exhorts him to be a man, to identify with him, and is even more worried than the mother about indulgence of his son, and about any evidence of sissyish behavior. Father and son begin to participate together in games and outings, often excluding females from their activities. But it is rarely possible that the modern father can permit his son to join him in his work.

To their mutual identification, mother and daughter can add mutual participation. Traditionally the little girl helped her mother with cooking, shopping and cleaning. Contemporary mothers often determine that their daughters shall not serve as housekeepers to their men, make a point of not teaching them these tasks, but instead play with them in projects of art or music or dance, and emphasize intellectual and language development.

Throughout latency, all children may continue to enjoy

some masturbation, but the girl's pleasure would seem more diffuse, less focal, than that of the boy, possibly less frightening. Playing with oneself is no longer sternly disapproved; thus diminished guilt and shame attach to the practice. Clinical data would suggest that the girl's phantasies are often quite loving ones and that the boy's phantasies, containing some rapacious themes, may be more troublesome to him. He is still anxiously reaching for what he feels is not rightfully his.

Freud (1931) noted that little girls are regularly more intelligent and livelier than boys of the same age, and that they form stronger attachments, but he dismissed these indications of what he considered a "difference in instinctual disposition" as "not of great consequence." In that era it was hardly questioned that males were destined to be the doers and makers, and so he could disregard these facts about females. The world still needed to exploit the power of males for purposes of conquering and building, exploring the frontiers, creating the industrial revolution. And it still required that woman should make anatomy her destiny.

To those boys who note that girls of the same age are superior in their schoolwork, their social poise, and their friendship patterns, the matter is very much of consequence. Some part of the motivation for that spontaneous separation of the sexes which we observe during latency is that girls feel superior to boys, and boys, secretly concurring, avoid that contact which would make this painful awareness of their envy inescapable. They profess to scorn girls' toys and activities, yet as any child therapist can attest, when in a situation which they feel to be safe, they indulge their secret wishes to play with dolls, doll houses, and other allegedly feminine toys. In this play we can often discern envy of the mother whom the boy sees as the source of all good things but who also has the power, and sometimes seemingly the intent, to deprive him or to favor a sibling. In his envy he projects his bad angry feelings onto the mother, and it frightens him that he may have destroyed her.

A defense perhaps more available to the boy is the intensification of genital desires and activity as a flight from orality (Klein, 1957). The accessibility of the penis makes it more possible for the boy to turn to compulsive masturbation as comfort for his oral grievances, and this may predispose him in later life to think of sex as a "need"—which way of thinking does appear more characteristic of the male. The urge to get rid of "noxious products" (Freud, 1923) may have psychic roots in the destructive envy of woman, the creator.

Sexual Changes and Exchanges in Adolescence

The boy has characteristically been slower than the girl in readiness for adolescent emotional exchanges, and our clinical data show males, even as adults, often being led or dragged into therapy by their women who want fuller mutual participation and communication. The boy's first sexual experiences have, in the past, tended to be with girls seen as "bad," about whom he cared not at all. There is evidence that this is changing as esteemed females award themselves greater sexual freedoms, but we still hear frequent female complaints that "all the boys want is sex!"

Complicating the integrating of sexuality into ego functioning is the recent lowering of the age of puberty. It is not unusual that a girl menstruates at ten, and some may do so even at eight or nine years. The onset of menarche can reactivate anxieties about sphincter control and about genital injury in girls who were predisposed by earlier trauma to sense of body self, or to excessive anxiety over loss of mother. Symptomatically such anxieties are evident in the veritable epidemic of anorexia we are witnessing. When the girl stops eating she manages to restore her body to some of its sexless preadolescent aspects; her menstruation stops and constipation occurs. A massive regression takes place which, among other effects, awakens the pregenital mother who must now concern herself once more with the nourishment and the toilet habits of her daughter.

For many girls, however, menstruation seems to be taken in stride. No longer is it called "the curse." Most of us note that young women talk of it more freely, both with us and with friends of both sexes, but we do not yet have data whether they speak of it as freely with male therapists as with female. We speculate that certain conveniences, such as tampons, may change the nature of the experience, and that prolific advertising has made menstruation an openly acceptable topic. Some feminist therapists go so far as to say that they never anymore hear of dysmenorrhea, painful menses. When the therapist is an outspoken women's libber, we might need to question the possible transference elements in patients never reporting such discomforts to her. Certainly in our practice there are women who suffer bloatedness, severe cramps, and shifts in mood. One of them recently carried on a diatribe against the medical profession that, in all these years, it has never come up with, or even searched for, suitable preventatives or remedies for this monthly malaise. It may be that the growing cadre of female physicians may attempt to solve these problems, as well as to meet the urgent need for safer contraceptives.

It would seem that most girls these days are actually eager to enter puberty when it does not come upon them too soon. When they have identified with an active mother, or sometimes a teacher, or a therapist, they may welcome the new challenges. Such girls are gratified that physical maturation no longer has to mean the cessation of aggression, the relinquishing of valued aspects of self. They see no reason to refrain from calling boys, or from taking the initiative in seeking them out, behaviors once thought to be forward and brash. They make friendships with males, and by mid-adolescence may even be traveling around the country or abroad in the companionship of both sexes and with parental consent. Rare is the girl who hides being an "A" student lest her intellectuality impede her popularity. And when such intellectuality is not primarily defensive and loaded with conflict, she does not forfeit her capacity for empathy, as Helene Deutch (1945) once warned.

As therapists we find ourselves still paying attention to the quality of mother-daughter ties in adolescence. We still see, as Peter Blos (1962) described, many girls who attach themselves to males in order to fight their ties to their mothers, and we note that they often pay a price, in that they then lose peer-group mothering. One patient was thus penalized when, at sixteen, she began a sexual relationship with a boy, and dropped or was dropped by all her female friends, which then, of course, reinforced her attachment to him. But she had a highly ambivalent relationship with her mother. She had been a child anxiously conceived, her mother on an anti-abortion drug during the pregnancy, the bearing of a baby essential to the mother's self-definition and intended to compensate for a decompensating marriage. Mother had had a post partum depression, and several later breakdowns, thus entailing hospitalization and separation from her daughter. The young girl felt it essential drastically to disentangle herself from a burdened and burdensome home background.

We might speculate that a former reason for the urgency with which the adolescent girl tried to break the tie with her mother was not just to throw off the shackles of dependency but to shed an identification with a weak passive mother, not a good model for the new woman. Many modern mothers, either with careers or with other absorbing interests of their own, do not foster dependency in their daughters, and may be highly esteemed by them. The old rebelliousness and battling are then hardly necessary.

There was a day when girls were labeled "delinquent" for behavior seen as normal in boys. Only a decade ago there were professionals (Walters, 1965) who declared that "premature sexual experimentation" would impair a girl's ego development. It is becoming more and more clear that we must redefine what we mean by premature, not loosely attaching it to age alone. Moreover, we might consider that the masculine ego traditionally has been retarded when his easy sexual discharge has been fostered by the culture, for the male often does not come to risk emotional interaction. The most common complaint we hear of wife against husband is that he is emotionally impotent.

The sexual experimentation of adolescents these days is not always confined to the opposite sex but includes, increasingly and fairly openly, homosexuality as well. Some psychoanalysts have expressed dismay over this, and have attributed it to the increasing tendency of fathers to play nurturing roles. Our guess is that, above all else, the fact that the world does not need more and more babies frees sexuality for purposes of other than procreation. It is used in play, and hence in the process of repair. The American Psychiatric Association can now decree that homosexuality is no longer to be considered pathological, and society can take a more tolerant view of that and other "perversions."

Although there always was a certain amount of sex play among members of the same sex, it used to be a source of nearly unbearable guilt and shame. We saw many patients, especially young men, in homosexual panics, and it was excruciatingly painful to them to confess, even to their therapists, their deeds or phantasies. Today we find that young people of both sexes speak almost as freely of their homosexual as of their heterosexual episodes, and, at least when the person is in therapy, there is an inclination to examine what reparative meanings those acts may hold at any given phase. This may well suggest a lesser probability of fixation to regressive behaviors and a greater likelihood that such experiments may be in the nature of self-provocations for the purpose of reworking old trauma (Shor, 1972).

It used to be thought that females were closer to homosexuality than were males (Freud, 1931) due to the former's long-standing tie to the mother. Certainly women have tended to be more comfortable with affection with each other, less threatened with what people would say should they even want to live together. Yet, although statistics are not available, it would appear that fewer women than men engage in overt homosexuality. The adolescent girls who a few years ago related in therapy their secret sexual experimentation with their female friends were for the most part rather consciously playfully exploring in lieu of, and as preface to, the as-yet-forbidden heterosexual relationships for which they yearned. Today some girls and women are turning to homosexuality out of repeated disappointments with non-expressive males, or out of a need to remedy psychic damage at the hands of, or perhaps we should say at the breast of, the preoedipal mother, the latter need usually less conscious than the first. This regression to a narcissistic mode of relationship has as its aim self-repair, and tends to be transitory when the patient can be conscious of its intent, and when she then can feel a sense of choice about it.

> Perhaps an illustration is in order. Bee, an eighteen-year-old, who for two years permitted herself to be in an exclusive relationship with a fellow whom she reluctantly saw as inferior to herself, recently reported what she termed an "orgy." She and her girlfriend each had intercourse with their respective boyfriends in the same bed, mutually observing, and then all four fondled each other. Bee permitted Sue to

"put her hand in me," and experienced orgasm. The meanings were on many levels. Bee's male friend had had an extended period of homosexuality before becoming involved with her, and her first jealousies about him were of that then not-quite-ended relationship. Her girl friend, Sue, had been telling her that she did not know a single person who wasn't "gay." So, on a conscious level, she wanted to discover what her peers were finding in their lesbian ways, what her boyfriend had experienced with his boyfriend. Less consciously, she was replaying an old trauma, that she had once had to renounce her father to live with her mother. Moreover, having done so, she had kept herself walled off from mother, whose psychotic character threatened the patient's own inner stability. She also rejected all girl friends in earlier adolescence, and clung to this boy. In her "orgy" Bee set things up so that she could turn to Sue, or we should say return, for Sue was one of the girl friends once discarded and now reclaimed, and could, without forfeiting her heterosexual tie, in this "safe" context, experience an opening-up, a moment of illusory merging with a female (mother). Thus the goal was to repair both oedipal and narcissistic damage.

The Further Reaches of Narcissism

It is clear that Blos' (1962) observation that the "biological events of puberty push the problem of masculinity and femininity into a final position" is no longer tenable. That consolidation of identity which used to occur in late adolescence is delayed, perhaps indefinitely. The longer time available means that the individual does not need to make his or her defects and constrictions part of character structure but can begin to discover in himself or herself new potentials.

But, tragically, as might be expected from the course of developments which we have outlined, men seem in a less favorable position to take advantage of the new options. That psychological fixity and rigidity which Freud (1931) once bemoaned as the state of a woman of thirty seems much more likely today in the male. Woman shows herself—into her forties or fifties and even later—capable of change, of adding the instrumental role which then permits her to develop further her expressive one. Having availed herself of the pill or the IUD, even though complaining of their now obvious hazards and imperfections, she now takes on education or training and goes forth into the world. Her narcissism is no longer tied up primarily with physical appearance and charm but is gratified more by her moving toward a new ideal of wholeness. And she is ready for new levels of relating.

When, however, she reaches to her husband for intimate sharing, she finds him too often unavailable and afraid. Although he may, in his chauvinistic ways, have promoted her freedom, he is still on his treadmill, unable to relinquish the ambitious striving upon which he has come to depend for narcissistic supplies, unable to open up and enjoy full mutuality. When his wife tries to persuade him to use the psychotherapy which she has found useful, he vigorously resists. He senses that it entails a regression which he has been trained to consider as forbidden and maybe dangerous. In our clinical experience, the married man may sometimes come to us when accompanied by his wife-mother, but for a long while he remains fearful of individual treatment.

There is heartening clinical evidence that the picture is changing, for younger and unmarried men are seen to be striving consciously for greater intimacy, and they enter treatment less fearfully, and perhaps in that spirit of self-provocation which is part of the intent of repair. There is reason to hope that females who have enjoyed such a favorable developmental course, and who feel a sense of choice about life's goals, will rear their sons and daughters more similarly, and will lead males to want to become more whole also. Then the traditional advantages and burdens may be de-intensified and shared more equally by both sexes (E. Balint, 1972).

"More whole" means, for each sex, transcending old allocated roles and freely partaking of prerogatives formerly reserved for the other sex, or, we might say, overcoming opposites. That woman has held the expressive role may once have derived from her biological function of pressing out, giving birth, and her subsequent communication to her baby via facial and other emotional gestures and vocal intonations, all of which were, unconsciously, part of her teaching her baby future expected role behaviors. Later she utilized these qualities in her verbal communication, being more facile than the male in expressing inner feelings and meanings. But she did not develop the power or the confidence directly to effect much in the world at large.

Man, on the other hand, possessed a "tool," an instrument by means of which he impregnated woman. But then he became an instrument himself, the means by which his family was fed, clothed and housed, the means by which society conquered nature, and nations conquered each other. To be aware of and indulge inner feelings could not be compatible with such ends (Shor, 1970).

Although there may be a phase in which women will be ahead of men in transcending former limitations, the stirring is toward a new equality. When each can claim for self the aspects and prerogatives formerly reserved for and hence projected on the other, they attain a fuller mutuality, characterized by strong identification with each other, enjoyment of similar activities and pursuits, and by rich communication at all levels, including that of deep inner feelings and thoughts.

The route for the needed repair is via play and illusion, as Winnicott and others of the British Psycho-analytic Society middle group have so well described. We have long been aware of the child's use of play as a way not only to allay anxiety, but to master trauma and to transform self by actively recreating situations once experienced passively. The illusory mastery so sampled permits further development to occur; thus the child becomes equipped to meet similar situations with new and more flexible responses. It is this same process utilized in adult therapy that enables the patient, male or female, to transcend former limitations imposed by both biology and culture.

As we take a fresh look at human development we may be moved to return to old myths whose truths we were not ready totally to grasp while we clung to our androcentric concepts. Apropos the issues we have pondered is the story of Narcissus, who was, as you know, not female, but male, and who perished of anorexia nervosa because he could not pull himself away from gazing at his beautiful reflection in the clear pool. A clinician interviewing his mother would have discovered that Narcissus was born a twin, but that his beloved twin sister had died in infancy. His mother, warned by a sage that she must never permit her son to see his own image or he would die, deprived him of that mirroring on which a cohesive sense of self depends (Kohut, 1971). He wandered about, as a young adolescent, unable to respond to the overtures of the nymphs, for he was lacking in capacity for empathy and warmth. In the pool he was transfixed to see at last the feminine side of himself, but when he reached in with his arms, again and again he came up empty-handed.

This classic myth portrays the pseudoautonomous male of our day who poses as self-sufficient. When he can begin to reach out for a phase of relating in which he can safely expose his deep dreads of rejection and destruction, then his efforts at self-repair may no longer be doomed to failure. His dilemma is the essential challenge for analytic psychotherapy with all patients.

Appendix B

Two Principles of Reparative Regression: Self-Traumatization and Self-Provocation *

by Joel Shor

Reprinted from THE PSYCHOANALYTIC REVIEW, Vol. 59, No. 2, 1972, through the courtesy of the Editors and the Publisher, National Psychological Association for Psychoanalysis, New York, N.Y.

Clinical concern with regression has been accelerating in all schools of analytic theory. Balint[7] has reviewed Freud's promptings and perplexities in this area. The recent renewal of interest in the theory of anxiety (Waelder, Rangell) and in the dynamics of trauma (Furst et al.) has advanced the recognition of potentially positive functions in some regressive experiences (Frosch et al. and Lindon et al.). Earlier publications by Ferenczi and Balint on the therapeutic uses of regression may now be re-examined with the rich equipment of more than three decades of both ego psychology and object-relations theory.

This report will attempt to develop and formulate some suggestions of theory and technique for two principles of constructive regression within character analysis, self-traumatization and self-provocation. An extended case example will illustrate the principles and procedures to be developed. I propose to view both principles as expressions of the discriminatory function of the ego (Hacker), with self-traumatization as a successful masochistic acting out, and with self-provocation as a successful repetition compulsion. Both types of success will be

---

* This paper is part of a chapter entitled "Illusion in Action" written for a book in preparation by the Research Division of the Southern California Psychoanalytic Institute, under the working title *Toward a Psychoanalytic Theory of Action,* edited by N. Tabachnick.

considered as manifestations of an even more basic principle of regression, that of reparation; the reparation of object relations by self-traumatization, and the reparation of narcissistic resources by self-provocation.

REGRESSION TO PRIMARY ILLUSION

As psychoanalytic theory and method progress to explore the phenomena of regression, within and without the therapeutic relationship, more and more formulations are being attempted concerning the earliest states of human experience and awareness. We see speculations about the preverbal stages of ego functioning deriving from "oceanic feelings" in a first, "undifferentiated phase" (Freud). The pioneers have long ago spoken of "the pre-ambivalent passive oral phase" (Abraham) and the stage of "passive object-love" (Ferenczi). Rank's leap to the birth trauma contains an intended and extended idealization of the fetal state. Groddeck heralds the primitive "It" forcing inherent models of organismic expression into all later relationships by somatic and symbolic processes. All analytic schools imply speculations about the first psychic state.

More recent developments of psychoanalysis have accelerated our awareness of and clinical concern with the primary psychic condition. We recognize this trend in the various names given to that state by Hartmann, Greenacre, Spitz, Erikson, Klein, Mahler, Jacobson, Benedek, Little, Fairbairn, Winnicott, Balint, and others: the early undifferentiated ego-id, basic security, basic trust, the idealized breast, the symbiotic pair, the perfect child-environment unit, primary object love, primary narcissism, basic unity, fusion, etc. I see a variety of new clinical approaches to this primary state in the work of Frosch, Kestenberg, Lowen, and Balint.

Of all these ways of conceptualizing the primary state, I wish to focus on the work of Balint. He has been offering a most consistent attention to the workings of the wish for primary unity in the clinical data of adult therapy, since his 1932 article, "Character Analysis and New Beginning." He also began there his speculations about the earliest awareness of being during the first weeks of existence. I quote his succinct description of the dynamics of that primary preverbal phase, also noting his clinical clues for patients' arriving at a constructively regressive state of "the new beginning":

> Primary love is a relationship in which only one partner may have demands and claims; the other partner (or partners, i.e., the whole world) must have no interests, no wishes, no demands, of his or her own. There is, and must be, a complete harmony, i.e., a complete identity of wishes and satisfactions. . . .[3]

And also:

> There is no fear inherent in the archaic object-love, only naive confidence and unsuspicious self-abandonment: the more paranoid and depressive anxieties and fears have been removed by analysis, the more clearly the phenomena of the archaic object-love—the new beginning in an adult patient—develop before our eyes.[1]

Thus from clinical data with adults and from speculation about the first state of human awareness, we are offered here a concept of the primary state that, I believe, remains the basic source, anchor, and model for all subsequent, uniquely human psychic developments. This hypothesis proposes an image of perfect and absolute harmony, effortless and timeless, with an easy flow and oscillation between autarchic (one-body) and relational (two-body) processes; and it assumes the persistence of this original and illusionary image as the core in the shaping for each person of his spiral of growth to death. With this formulation, I believe Balint[7] resolves several issues separating traditional theories of primary narcissism from the newer object-relations theories. It is the concept of *illusion* which bridges the gap; not hallucination or delusion, but simply illusion. In Ferenczi's *Thalassa* we are offered a speculative framework for the role of illusion in the human condition.

Many other writers since Ferenczi have favored this view of illusion as intrinsic to man's management of himself and his world. For instance, Winnicott provides clinical and developmental details of the inevitable and constructive processes of illusion in his writings about transitional object, play, and creativity. Even closer formulations of the specific issue of the inherent role of illusion are given by Milner[37] and Rycroft.[46] Schafer has explored developmental aspects of related processes using illusions in his "Ideals, Ego Ideal, and Ideal Self" (chapter in Holt[24]). Ross identifies some benign aspects and forms of illusion in "as if" phenomena. Also pertinent is Huizinga's[26] historical study of the play-element in culture. Hacker[21] broadens this view into a concept of the constructive and inevitable role of myth-making and myth-revising in human history and individual development. His hypotheses about myth have central relevance to our concept of illusion and its functioning for reparation and renewal.

In a short paper[48] about a statue in Freud's garden, I attempted to suggest the role of illusion in mediating between Eros (tenderness) and Thanatos (aggression), with speculations for a bioneural basis for the primary illusion. I quote from that paper:

> Primary narcissism begins with the ultimate dilemma; the "eternal" human ego emerges from and rests on a time-bound material body. and the psyche must battle the biological death principle. A precarious victory is won by fantasies of megalomanic omnipotence, but these are beaten to new shapes by reality.

In this battle there are phases of mock victory, when several deeply necessary illusions can be identified. I now believe that these images may prove to be clinical patterns that could stimulate laboratory investigations of neurological processes and of the ultimate mysteries of neural tissue (Pribram[39,40]).

There are forerunners in Freud's work to this relationship between regression and illusion. He prepares us to consider regression as a source of basic hope and basic energies in his recognition of its "origin . . . in the helplessness of childhood," and its persistence "into maturity" (*New Introductory Lectures,* p. 229). He encourages our positive concern with infantile illusions underlying action and fantasy in his *Future of an Illusion*:

> Thus we call a belief an illusion when wish fulfillment is a prominent factor in its motivation. . . . the illusion need not be necessarily false, that is to say, unrealizable or incompatible with reality [p. 54].

PLAY AND THE SENSE OF EFFORT: REPARATIONS OF THE PRIMARY ILLUSION

"Illusion . . . means literally 'in play' " (Huizinga[26]). The sense of play provides essential clues to the conscious experience of primary love: the qualities of spontaneity and effortlessness. In the state of primary love, action occurs, but there is little delay of gratifications, little frustration of wishes or intentions, only the momentary awareness of an impulse meeting satisfaction. However, inevitable failures extend the moments of delay and yield a supply of unbound, unmet energies that work to form ego structures. It is these developments that foster the sense of effort and the control of action. And it is neural and muscular maturation that make ready, and prompt, the experience of effort against the backdrop of the inevitable failure of effortless primary love.

During these early phases of development, the parents (source) foster the illusionary process by their megalomanic reassurances appropriate to the child's inevitable feelings of desperate dread and total disaster, such as a mother's saying, "I'll kiss it and make it better." Parents and society continue to promise the child supplies, aims, and objects so as to sustain the illusory hope for primary love.

Such double-binding messages are inevitable, but the subjective degrees of conflict and confusion will determine how much stimulation or paralysis derives from the inherent dialectic of complaint and promise. The private measures of pain and of constructive provocations are the burden of individuality, which we face so centrally in our clinical work. Yet the culturally directed stages of development are attempts at reparation, and preparation; they serve as contexts and containers, as substitutes and detours for the original and ultimate illusion (Erikson,[11] Tabachnick[54]).

PRIMARY ILLUSION IN ADULT LOVE AND THERAPY

Balint[1] reminds us that the "supreme happiness" of "mystical union" between adults in genital sex and love

> is to a very large extent illusion, based on regression to an infantile stage of reality testing. This primitive reality testing permits the individual to believe—for a short time—that all his needs have been satisfied, that the whole world, in particular everything good in the world, is the happy *Me*. . . . Healthy people are elastic enough to experience this far-going regression without fear, and with complete confidence that they will be able to emerge from it again . . . unscathed or even thrilled and refreshed.

Balint's[3] principle is "progression for the sake of regression." His view transcends Kris' classical formula, "regression in the service of the ego." Balint's formulation advances the challenge put by Freud in his article "On the Split of the Ego in the Defensive Process" (1938). There, Freud sees fantasy fulfillment and reality mastery as "two contrary reactions, both valid and effective. . . . [This] rift in the ego . . . increases as time goes on."

The experience of oneness in mature love, in mutual orgasm, is the product of a dialogue between two persons feeling essentially and comfortably whole and separate, and yet communicating on both verbal and nonverbal levels of contact. The dialogue develops an increasing number of regressed symbolic identifications ("illusions") and behavioral accomodations ("realities"). Complementarity of response accelerates spontaneously into a sense of primary unity, of fusion. The mutuality includes processes of identification, participation, and communication, all moving toward moments of maximum psychological and physiological unity (Shor[49]). It advances by private and subjective measures of feelings and forces, in self and the other. These measures are open to error and illusion.

Each person seeks experiences of confirmation and affirmation, alternating adaptively. Both "aspects of identity formation" (Tabachnick[54]) are necessary for a constructive growth experience. The confirmations will depend on object-relations processes; the affirmations emerge from instinctual forces (Spitz[53]) or "narcissistic resources." The array of needs to be met for each adult partner includes ongoing drives as well as fixations and residues from earlier phases of life. This mutual regression becomes a spiral process, relying upon realistic strengths earned separately and then shared. This sharing experience becomes a smooth, continuous, flexible flow between two states: one-person complete (autarchic, megalomanic "Me," secure in its primary narcissistic supplies) and two-person ("I-You" object-relation) (Balint[2]).

As in adult loving, the patient's regression toward primary love transference in psychoanalysis evokes acting within an illusion of absolute harmony and security. Such transference regressions to nonverbal levels of expression follow successful meetings (transference analysis) on the verbal level. A present piece of "working out" the therapeutic alliance precedes working through the specific and implicit cores of the character neurosis (Karush[28]). Spontaneous regressions, of course, occur in the earliest phases of analysis, but the patient may not be ready to usefully risk further regression to the primary illusion. He must first experience substantial gains in ego autonomy from the interpretive analysis of the transference.

With each successful, regressive glimpse of the primary illusion there are revived the yet unresolved infantile wishes specific to each patient. He then re-experiences his characteristic conflicts and defenses in the context of his revitalized reparative aims. New confrontations occur, with fresh efforts for a working-through of the instinctual components in conflict. Thus he resumes that dialectic of complaint and promise necessary for his psychic growth.

Balint identified such "new beginnings" in 1932, and he offered details of specific clinical processes and technical procedures in 1968. The sequence of clinical phases, as I see them, oscillating between verbal and nonverbal expressions of the same specific problem, will be illustrated later in the case example.

SELF-MEASUREMENT, CHOICE, AND THE DECISION TO ACT

Throughout the therapeutic process we can recognize the oscillation between the impulses toward regression and progression. The pace of the analytic process is guided by the patient's subjective measures of the forces and resources at stake. Transference analysis is our major tool to assist him to improve his measurements of the threats and pressures from object relations and their internal representations. This is classical method. However, it becomes a further task to measure the damages and dangers in the area of his narcissistic resources. Here we first trust to his private estimates, following the qualitative clues we give in our interpretations of defenses against instinctual components (Money-Kyrle[38]). But when these classical methods fail, as the case will illustrate, we may abandon our efforts, or we may risk proceeding more directly. Continuing therapy may move us to direct his subjective attention to his yet unverbalized or unverbalizable feelings and sensations. We cannot interpret further until the patient has become aware of these unconscious components, which he then must assess.

The question arises: has man evolved special private processes for these internal measurements and balancings? Both the act of decision and the decision to act imply such functions, in the face of the inherent privacy and subjectivity in awareness. The internal task is inevitable, though Freud has warned us: "Mental events seem to be immeasurable and probably will always be so."* Rapaport[43] alerts us to the complexities of measuring affect, "the instinctual discharges into the interior." Rangell[41] presents us with further considerations but encourages us to respect and value the challenge of the private "human core." Schafer[47] also has warned us of the continuing ambiguities in seeking precision in "the clinical analysis of affects."

For this central task, also, Hacker[20] has focused on the workings of the "discriminatory function of the ego." Discrimination requires the capacity to assert "No" to an instinctual impulse and its derivatives (Spitz[53]). I consider that the decision to act is precipitated from the balancing of clearer negations permitting safer affirmations. (For metapsychology, negations may be the source of the concept of the death principle, as well as the core of the mechanism of repression). The crucial clinical aim remains, as in all analytic therapy, to increase self-awareness and ego-syntonic participation in the measurement of affects, functions, and resources. The balancing of subjective measurements of inner and outer forces for and against each act yields a choice or decision, as against a trauma or accident.

Some further support for this approach may be seen in recent studies of dreaming, of the rapid-eye-movement period of sleep. These researches have been reviewed by Dement and Fischer.† I focus on

---

* Quoted in Ernest Jones, *The Life and Work of Sigmund Freud,* Vol. 2 (New York, Basic Books, 1957), p. 419.

† Psychoanalytic Implications of Recent Research on Sleep and Dreaming (*Journal of the American Psychoanalytic Association,* Vol. 13, 1965), pp. 197-303.

their discovery of a regular, universal phenomenon of withdrawing in sleep to experience one's own internal forces, drives, and anxieties without the dangers of discharges in external action. The detailed REM data show that these affects are allowed to overrun the vital and expressive functions and organs of the person, including dream-making, but not the larger musculature required in firm, direct action on the outer world. I suggest that these REM periods of restricted expression may be useful phases preparatory to a private, subjective measure of the psychic forces, and preliminary to decisions about the world of overt action in the service of the reality principle. Lerner[33] has developed a closely related hypothesis as applied to dreaming and Rorschach responses. In fact, in 1919, Ferenczi had anticipated such dramatic, muscular processes as a consequence of and a cause for further human evolution, and as preparation for a normal function of fantasy:

> In hysterical symptoms we see—to our no small amazement—that organs of vital importance subordinate themselves entirely to the pleasure principle, regardless of their own particular function in reality. . . . The musculature, instead of as usual assisting us in the maintenance of life by purposively coordinated activities, exhausts itself in dramatic representations of the pleasurable situations of phantasy. . . . Now I do not believe that we are dealing here with processes that hold good for hysteria only, and are otherwise meaningless or generally absent. Certain processes in normal sleep indicate that phantastic materialization-phenomena are also possible in people who are not neurotic [*Further Contributions,* p. 103].

SELF-PROVOCATION IN DELIBERATE ACTING-OUT

Alongside the possibility that man has evolved his largely subjective processes for measuring the self- or ego-syntonic excitement, the pleasure and the anxiety already developed internally, I wish to suggest that he has also learned to risk, regularly, a process of acting-out to test and measure alien or dystonic forces, external realities. Kleinian theory has formulated the projective processes for the repair of the damaged object. I add now the view that we are also intent on repairing damaged parts of the narcissistic self. Both reparative aims do indeed overlap in any clinical moment, but the balance of emphasis can be differentiated by clarifying the working alliance at that point. To develop this approach to the function of action in ego growth, I quote four paragraphs from my "Self Provocation and Reparation": *

* Paper presented to the British Psycho-Analytic Society, February 1963.

The process of evoking new types of confrontation has in fact always been in the nature of the therapeutic workings of transference analysis. Anna O. literally insisted upon Breuer's patient attendance according to her pace and measure of tension, and she thus initiated the psycho-analytic situation and its particular ethic. ("The Ethic of Freud's Psycho-Analysis," *International Journal of Psycho-Analysis,* 1961). The further progress of analytic method and theory depends upon the continued insistence of our patients and their demands for deeper self-knowledge. . . .

In a previous publication ("Ego Development Through Self-Traumatization," *Psychoanalytic Review,* 1953, with M. L. Coleman) clinical examples were given of children provoking their parents to manifest hostile attitudes in the hope of externalizing these "bad objects" and thus achieving a clearer perspective for further ego defense. During analysis as adult patients, they came to learn how such provocations emerged from their unconscious dreads about their parents' unconscious attitudes. The provocative incidents had occurred between the ages of six and twelve years and were persistently recalled during treatment as justification for character weaknesses. These "screen memories" were repeated until the provocative aim was interpreted. Similar provocations were expressed in the transference; this time analysis permitted the patient to recall and reconstruct the reparative aims concealed behind the long-standing screen memories of these crucial traumatic events. In these cases the exposure of parental hostility had resulted in a fresh trauma too severe to allow the child then to recognize consciously his wish to repair the parent.

Another publication ("A Well-Spring of Psycho-analysis," *Psychoanalysis,* 1953) suggested that reparation is part of the aim of all creative activity, including the usefully narcissistic aspects of a fuller maturity. When object relations fail, the reparative aim may include efforts to repair oneself, as well as the repairing of bad or destroyed objects. Character neuroses are especially likely to contain damaged body ego functions: these weaknesses may be bound up with layers of never verbalized dread about lasting damage to one's functions of instinctual expression. Here too, analysis may facilitate a process of self-provocation in the patient, so that he evokes in himself more of these anxieties obstructing his possession and use of deeper narcissistic resources. (This is the principle of character analysis.)

Self-provocation is an experiment, a testing of reality, inner reality. When the provocation fails to allow a working through to a better position for ego defense, the attempt has usually been called a "repetition compulsion" or a "masochistic acting-out"; both terms have been identified as expressions of Freud's Death Instinct. A successful self-provocation will lead to the relinquishing of a bad introject, and the establishing of a stronger narcissistic phase, in preparation for a better pattern of object relationship. In this sense, a successful self-provocation is a constructive acting-out. The consciously self-directed acting-out may yield a discharge of anxiety about an instinctual component, and allow the patient to make a clearer measure of his pain or pleasure, and their origins. Such knowledge equips the ego for a more precise management of its sources and resources, and fosters the spiral of creative and flexible ego development.

The test for these hypotheses will be in the development of more effective clinical methods in character analysis. Major clinical concerns emerge: the management of spontaneous regressions from the working alliance, and the working-through of the transference complications from the specific parameters beyond classical method. The case illustration, however, will focus primarily on the action-methods which emerged from the unresolved conflicts liberated by classical technique. The principle of self-arousal of affect is to be interwoven, at the patient's pace, with the larger principle of transference-resistance analysis. The self-provoked feelings may evoke affective, self-syntonic awarenesses of memories and reconstructions, which facilitate effective, abreactive working-through of the basic character conflicts. En route, we each, privately, learn the nonverbal bodily sensations that presage the neurotic processes. The basic therapeutic aim remains: to transfer the acting-out impulses from outside to inside the clinical situation and thus to subject the sources of these impulses to deeper, existential character-analytic treatment. The therapeutic process of working-through is dependent upon the idealization of and identification with the analyst's real qualities as expressed within the working out of the transference neurosis.[8,27,28,29]

To this classical idea, I add the principle of self-renewal of the patient's hopes for regression to the primary illusion, and the technical method of self-provocation. The parameters aim to make ego-syntonic character defenses ego-alien at an effective nonverbal depth. The criterion of clinical progress remains: increased affective, private awareness and insight, with the appearance of new instinctual discharges, in action or affect-expression, under an economy of more abundant and flexible ego structures. Such advances may be achieved more safely first within the analytic session.

ACTIVITY PARAMETERS: MEASURES FOR REGRESSION

Ferenczi's work "On Forced Phantasies" first proposes a parameter to provoke directly the report of fantasies and feelings privately implicit to a spontaneous free association. He recommends the verbal intervention "And then?" as a pressure for fuller details of defenses and drives in conflict. He suggests from these new data that "A certain amount of infantile sexual experience [that is to say, a little "sexual traumatism"] not only does not damage but actually promotes the later normality, particularly the normal activity of phantasy." Ferenczi identifies a dialectic of crises as inherent to human psychic development. Abraham had offered a cue to this view in his 1907 study of dementia praecox (Furst[17]).

Ferenczi[13] proceeded to experiments with the development of an "active therapy." First he explored the usefulness of prohibitions of bodily functions as an extension of Freud's principle of abstinence. When these measures failed to evoke sufficiently effective awareness and reflections, he began to explore the dimensions of "indulgence" of action-impulses by suggestions of muscle relaxation. These developments are also reported by Balint.[6,7]

Balint recognizes the potential value of expanding classical psychoanalysis beyond its verbal limits into nonverbal expression and the deprivation-indulgence principles, but he emphasizes the larger principle of the analytic ethic, that the patient himself regulates these measures for decision and action, in his "Character Analysis and New Beginning" (1932):

> That is the crucial point: that the amount of excitation, the degree of tension, is actually determined by the patient himself. This explains why in many cases the otherwise useful interventions (such as those recommended by Ferenczi) remain ineffectual.

This crucial consideration may allow a fuller use of the related "autogenic training" tradition (Hoppe[25]) within character analysis. The problems in the use of parameters (Eissler[10]) must be noted. Yet experienced patients' pressures to regress for self-reparation encourage us to confront the clinical complications in using parameters. Clinically we recognize some of the ways action within psychoanalysis may temporarily disperse defensive structures or conceal components of instinctual energies, and so evade a useful verbalization about impulses, motives, and anxieties.[27,29] Yet it is the realm of bodily sensations that can suggest both the nascent intention and the incipient action. Thus we may deepen and enlarge the field of awareness of hidden forces.

Freud posed the problem directly in his *Ego and Id,* pointing to the tasks in developing a language of bodily sensations: "The ego is first and foremost a body ego . . . ultimately derived from bodily sensations." Then he alerts us to some difficulties in reading and communicating a language of body expressions for our task of formulating hypotheses about nonverbal levels of experience. He advances these general concerns in the appendices to *Inhibitions, Symptoms, and Anxiety* (Waelder[55]).

Freud had very early anticipated the clinical problem of nonverbal expression of affect. In an 1899 letter to Fliess, he wrote:

> From time to time I visualize a second part of the method of treatment—provoking patients' feelings as well as their ideas, as if that were quite indispensable.

Patients increasingly come to complain about their own character traits, especially experienced patients, as the case will illustrate. The emergence of character analysis from the 1930's promised much progress in method and theory of modifying character neuroses. Reich (1960) and his disciples fail by abandoning the analytic ethic of self-determination, as well as by their disregard and disrespect for the degrees of autonomous power of psychic structures as they develop beyond their bioenergetic sources. Reich presumed a naive ideal of perfect, instinctual harmony in human nature; Freud, and Balint, accept a human condition that is never finished but subject to significant modification by man's rational ego developments. Yet the current disillusionment with psychoanalysis may be related in part to our delay in developing character analytic method to match our deepening theories about the preverbal and nonverbal aspects of health and pathology. Balint[3] states:

> What we need above all is more knowledge about the patient's imperative need to regress and the meaning of the various ways that patients use during regression.

A CLINICAL APPLICATION

The case example is from the analysis of a 42-year-old man who had twelve years of previous analytic treatment. My purpose is simply to illustrate some of the procedures for increasing awareness of the levels of feelings and body sensations by deliberate affect-expression activities within the specific clinical context of character analysis.

He was a member of the faculty in the Social Science Department of a university. His presenting complaint was a feeling of hopelessness about ever being at home in any professional position or in any intimate personal relationship with a man or woman. He traced the history of his difficulties and of his previous treatments in great detail.

He had begun treatment at age 20, having been working on a sociological project studying the street gangs of boys in a large city when his supervisor "informed" him that he was a latent homosexual and sent him to the university psychiatrist. He had a year of work with the psychiatrist, then was referred to a "Freudian" analyst, where he had six years of therapy. After a pause of about two years, he worked with an analyst of a "neo-Freudian" school of psychiatry for nearly two years. This was followed very soon after by more than a year with a "Reichian" analyst. At age 36, he returned to his first analyst, reviewed his situation, and accepted referral to a colleague, also a "Freudian character analyst." Three years of work here, and then his psychoanalyst referred him to me because of my experimental approach to such "experienced" patients. He worked with me for one and a half years.

At the time he began work with me, he had been engaged for some four or five years in the practice of picking up boy hitchhikers and leading them, through light conversation, to look at some pictures which he kept on hand. These were mostly photographs of boys of puberty age in poses of being bound and tortured. He then asked them to make up stories about these pictures, and while observing the emotional responses of the boys, the professor would have a secret ejaculation if the boy's reactions or their stories moved him to tender feelings. The patient was also frequently challenging his professional superiors and contriving to have to change his position of work; the issue at stake overtly was his extreme insistence on the principles of giving young people more freedom in school, at home, and in their social and sexual life.

I would like to give examples of the self-provocative procedures that emerged in the course of my working with this patient, usually three sessions per week. These will be extreme examples, and the stages before we arrived at these phases will be omitted. While risking the use of these parameters, I continued to try to be aware of the transference-resistance complications and to analyze them as soon as I recognized them. We had a well-developed working alliance.

In the course of therapy, a sequence of three specific procedures emerged, each of which led spontaneously to the next. These were applied to three layers of defense, each against fully experiencing and expressing the previous level of character defense. In this case each one yielded some new affective awareness of defensive reactions and thus advanced the analysis to some degree.

The first procedure emerged from his renewed awareness of wishes to destroy his mother and of feelings of intense and violent fury, which he was never able to express to his satisfaction. He had frequently elaborated on these ideas in his previous treatments. We too failed to modify these destructive wishes, despite several cycles of classically interpreting his illusory fear of losing mother completely. He remained attached to an impotent demand to experience his full fury. He realized the dangers and damages from his acting out at work and in society. I now added the interpretation that he wished to repair his expressive functions, so long paralyzed, as part of the primary love state; but he insisted that he wanted only to discharge this fury safely and "be done with it." His persistence led us to our first parameter, related to Darwin's[9] first principle, the deliberate exaggeration of emotional expressions (1872).

When the patient demanded his freedom for fuller discharge of his anger, I interpreted with firmness his projections of threatening and oppressive power and intent, as though I controlled his body functions. He accepted the liberating hint in the transference comment, and called on me to be his ally, to show him how to do it. I interpreted this benign projection with gentleness. He looked about neutrally, then sadly, and said: "I don't know how to do it. Can you help me? How do you do it?" I replied that I was not feeling any anger but that I knew how to express it when I decided to do so. And I added that I would be willing to observe his attempts in the session, within limits which I would try to foresee, and I would offer comparisons and suggestions to the details of his efforts.

The analytic working alliance was explicitly extended to his spontaneous explorations for meeting his own demand for freer, fuller self-expression, including some nonverbal aspects. He proceeded to make suggestions of ways to experience his anger and to ask my specific restrictive limits. To such direct requests, I replied in practical, realistic terms, not with further transference analysis at this time. Yet I remained alert to any distortions of these qualities of objective cooperation; when they occurred, I returned to interpreting the transference.

He came to suggest that he stand beside the couch and literally work up his anger by pummeling and pounding the couch; during these exertions he considered my observations about his posture, movements, and breathing, *if he felt they were obstructing his immediate reparative aim of ridding himself of his blocked anger.* Sometimes he spontaneously screamed as he pounded with his fists. Through a flexible series of attempts he increased his capacity to discharge his anger, especially if he allowed himself to breathe more easily. Slow, gentle breathing prepared him to assume more completely angry postures and assisted his measure of his feelings of readiness to act, to strike the couch.

In the midst of one attempt he was overwhelmed with frantic anger. He collapsed onto the couch and broke into powerful gasping spasms of crying. Then he spoke again, with much feeling, about his sense of futility and fright about ever discharging his anger completely. He saw himself blocked in a rigidly and defiantly aggressive position. From this "stuck" position, we returned to analytic interpreting before arriving at our next procedure, a parameter that illustrates Darwin's second principle, "antithesis, or exaggeration of the opposite emotional expressions."

When he regained his composure after the crying outburst, I focused on interpreting his helpless rigidity. He recalled several incidents in which he felt his need for help from his father. He recalled memories of enjoying mutual sensitivities with his mother, which were lacking in his relationship with his father. I repeated the theme of his wish for primary love. The next several sessions yielded more vivid associations to tenderness from his mother, but then also her sudden failure to accept his assertive tendencies. She constricted his attention and spontaneity by her own defensive gentleness, as she had done to his father. Thus she allowed only gentle activities and attitudes. His repressed assertive feelings gathered into fantasies of violence and torture, as we identified them in his apparently homosexual activities, and in his failure to ever allow an ejaculation in the knowing presence of another person. The underlying fear was seen to be that of being trapped in a tender, needing state, with no tolerance for assertiveness, especially with mother figures. This included all women of potential heterosexual interest to him. He had never had a complete sexual act with a woman though he had been to bed with a woman colleague on several occasions.

A second parameter evolved. The analytic material allowed him to focus on his feelings of constriction when reaching to mother for help. He could not risk feelings of basic trust.

Seeing this dilemma in his efforts with me, he agreed to risk reaching for the needy feelings, not the anger. He assumed the posture of an infant literally reaching up and calling out, "Help me, please help me, I need you." Again, my comments about his posture, voice quality, and breathing were attended to, and he slowly increased the degree of ego-syntonic affect in his attempts. Several times he broke into fury and gave up in despair. However, he came to resume his efforts, and discovered, especially through experimenting with a more relaxed breathing out, that the expression of needing and wanting help evoked a strong feeling of nausea and rejection.

The nausea would become intense and stopped his wish to experience his feelings of dependency. He recalled incidents with his mother in which he became confused at the sudden change from the sense of a pleasurable outing to one of oppressive isolation. He also remembered his efforts to find identification with his father, which had failed and left him damaged.

A third procedure emerged. We reviewed this cycle of reaching for help and failing because of feelings of nausea. His persistence, despite failure, encouraged us to be ready to provoke more complete, actual expressions of the feelings of nausea. I obtained a suitable pan and told him it was available. He explored by gently stimulating the back of his tongue and nearby throat linings to produce the beginning of a gag reflex.

We proceeded cautiously and I reminded him to remain alert to the two danger signals which I had by this time learned to consider as firm signs that such provocations of body sensations must stop at once. These two signals were a feeling of dizziness or fainting, and sudden pain in any part of the body. Also I was especially attentive to the patient's ease of breathing and of sighing while attempting to provoke the nauseated feelings. The making of sound vibrations helped to produce a fuller experience of affect. I again was alert to the dangers of hyperventilation. At this time, no such complications arose.

He made a series of attempts and gradually came to tolerate some strong nausea, and several times brought up small amounts of stomach contents. His tolerance of these distasteful sensations, self-provoked, increased his awareness of his feelings of ambivalence toward the mother image. He would allow himself to reproduce this dilemma of conflicting sensations of nausea and frequently stopped provoking them and proceeded to free associate. He recalled specific examples of being trapped by his mother's subtly guiding him into sharing her delicate, passive, wounded feminine sensitivities; and her equally subtly seducing him away from his independent and assertive intentions and expressions. For example, he recalled her device of confusing him by "sweetly" informing him—"You don't really think this," and "You don't really feel that, do you?" Also, her way of pursuing him by double-binding questions such as, "I don't think you *want* to do that, do you?"

The patient associated to thoughts about his upper-class mother's fear and disgust toward her husband's "crude" middle-class masculine manners and movements. The patient also recognized his conflicting identifications with *both* parents in the stalemate problem of his mother's feelings, her ambivalence about being penetrated by the father's harsh and inferior penis. I believe it was this stalemate of opposed sensations and feelings that had been blocking his analysis. These were not completely new ideas to him, but he said he *felt* more convinced of their truth for him. The activated body sensations in my presence furthered the working-through. He could trust the friendly neutrality of transference analysis.

The analysis proceeded to work through these ideas into the details of his fantasies and feelings about and in his homosexual activities. He renewed his reparative aims for his freedom of expression and possession of his own good resources. These had been displaced onto the youngsters in his sexual escapades, and the new protest movements among student "hippies." He slowly redefined his task of making over his sense of identity by making more of a home base in himself.

These three self-provocative procedures were flexibly explored over several weeks near the end of my work with this patient. We stopped treatment because of my long-standing plans to move to another city. It is my impression that the specific gains from these experiments were major factors in his stopping his homosexual excursions and remaining in the same professional position beyond a second year full of crises. More basically, he began to settle into a new flat and to make it more completely his own home. Beyond this, I can, at best, only anticipate that he may be achieving more satisfaction of his reparative goals, through useful narcissistic expressions, as a preliminary to his reaching for object relations at a more mature level. My intent here is simply to give illustrations of the principle of self-provocation of body sensations and action-awareness in depth through these extreme examples, and thus to propose principles for developing character analytic method to master more of the nonverbal defenses and resistances.

SOME METHODOLOGICAL ASSUMPTIONS AND METAPSYCHOLOGICAL ISSUES

The case illustration surely provokes questions about clinical method and principle. It is, of course, possible that another analyst working with other theories and interpretive procedures might have achieved equal or better therapeutic effects without the use of any activity parameters. Such speculations are relevant but difficult to test. The variables are many and subtle. However, in the interest of clarifying some of these variables, and in anticipation of further, fuller publications of the rationale of these activity methods, I list here some major assumptions underlying the use of expressive-action parameters:

1. Human action is a precipitate of instinctual derivatives fused into ego-syntonic moments, through basic character defenses. The impulses and energies which are discharged can be identified in the details of the action, including the verbalizable elements of awareness (thoughts, feelings, fantasies, images, and sensations) as well as the nonverbal muscular-neural expressive gestures. The clinical principle is to attend to the oscillation of these verbal and nonverbal expressions in close alternation and then to interpret the transference distortions of the character neurosis. The clinical consequence may be an increase in preconscious ego-flexibility beyond character rigidities.

2. The tendency toward regression contains both reparative and self-reparative components that seek to equip the ego apparatus with an increasing flexibility to merge into timeless moments of illusion of primary love. We expect a series of self-paced suspensions of object relatedness for improving one's narcissistic resources. We derive our focus on psychological reparative processes from the long-established medical facts of physiological reparation. The specific, psychic reparative aims should be included as part of each interpretation of the defensive character compromise evident in the transference. The basic blocks to constructive, benign regression are paranoid-schizoid and depressive terrors (Klein[31]).

3. The regressions proceed at a pace and through pathways subject to the patient's private assessment of his impulses and their defenses. The analyst's task here is essentially to focus the patient alternately on the verbal and nonverbal details of the neurotic process. By this principle of alternating attention, we aim to liberate a maximum flexibility of the patient's awareness and expression of his own measures of anxiety and pleasure. Thus he may be able to assume more aware responsibility for his decisions to act and their consequences. Transference interpretations will precede and follow these phases of self-directed explorations of awareness. Careful character analysis permits us to see how each psychic component influences, in details, the pattern of the overt act.

4. Fundamental to the use of activity procedures, or of any parameters, is the need for increasing alertness to and flexibility about

the transference and countertransference distortions. Forepleasure part-object discharges are likely to occur, such as hand-holding, and if accepted along with immediate analytic interpretation they prevent accumulations of unbearable tensions which would disrupt the working alliance.[6,7] Some qualities of genital maturity in the analyst are a prerequisite, a protective container, an implicit model, and the source of insights for the patient's progress towards his own fuller maturity. As always, the use of such parameters in clinical method are influenced by the real qualities of the analyst,[28] including the limits, in degree and areas, of his own ego flexibilities (Greenson[18]). The open admission and acceptance of such personal limits, when confronted by the patient, will help to protect the therapeutic value of the deeply and inherently existential quality in transference analysis.

5. A clinical approach to nonverbal experience requires some concepts and hypotheses to bridge patterns of energy processes and object relations. The theoretical starting points proposed for a renewal of instinct psychology are the three classical phases of instinctual energy functioning as formulated by Freud: source, aim, and object. Each phase provides a new, next quality of relating to the external world. Each phase provokes a different type of trauma, conflict, and crisis in character development:

> *Source* trauma: *deprivation* of basic supplies—failure of basic trust (object as original source)
>
> *Aim* trauma: *suppression* of free efforts—failure of assertive autonomy (object as container)
>
> *Object* trauma: *frustration* of bound energies—failure of interpersonal exchange (object as focus of discharge)

6. Clinical regression to states of *frustration* will require the purely classical transference analysis. Regressions to pre-Oedipal *deprivation* and *suppression* crises may require particular action parameters that revive the traumatic cores of earlier character fixations. The preverbal and nonverbal bonds and strains in these regressions are a serious challenge for abreactive working-through within character analysis. The sense of effort and of conscious intention must be "de-automatized" (Brodsky[8]) to permit changes in psychic structures, to allow new ego defenses to develop. Balint[6,7] reports clinical criteria and processes observed in meeting and facilitating these regressions within psychoanalysis. Underlying such risks is the assumption of a well-developed working alliance with the experienced patient.

7. Self-traumatization is inherent in the classical transference neurosis. The process of self-provocation may follow, within the working alliance, if the patient is permitted to regress to pre-Oedipal faults in his character development.

8. Freud alerts us (in "The Splitting of the Ego in the Defensive Process," 1938) to "something new and puzzling." He advises that our one-sided emphasis on ego synthesis has been "clearly at fault" and offers the summary consideration that normal development may require "a rift in the ego which never heals but which increases as times goes on." He suggests that

> there is a conflict between the demand of the instinct and the command of reality . . . the two contrary reactions to the conflict persist as the centre-point of a split in the ego.

I interpret this human condition as a built-in provocation toward an ego flexibility that increases its mastery over reality to ultimately allow its freer fantasy-laden responses to instincts. Balint[3] has advanced this perspective in his formulation, "Progression for the sake of Regression."

REFERENCES

1. BALINT, M. *Primary Love and Psychoanalytic Technique.* London: Hogarth Press, 1952.
2. ————. The Three Areas of the Mind. *International Journal of Psycho-Analysis,* Vol. 39, 1958.
3. ————. *Thrills and Regressions.* New York: International Universities Press, 1959.
4. ————. Primary Narcissism and Primary Love. *Psychoanalytic Quarterly,* Vol. 29, 1960.
5. ————. The Regressed Patient and His Analyst. *Psychiatry,* Vol. 23, No. 3, 1960.
6. ————. The Malignant and Benign Forms of Regression. In G. S. Daniels (Ed.), *New Perspective in Psychoanalysis.* New York: Grune and Stratton, 1965.
7. ————. *The Basic Fault: Therapeutic Uses of Regression.* London: Hogarth Press, 1968.
8. BRODSKY, B. Working Through: Its Widening Scope and Some Aspects of Its Metapsychology. *Psychoanalytic Quarterly,* Vol. 36, 1967.
9. DARWIN, C. *The Expression of Emotions in Man and Animal.* New York: Basic Books, 1872.
10. EISSLER, K. R. The Effect of the Structures of the Ego on Psychoanalytic Technique. *Journal of the American Psychoanalytic Association,* Vol. 1, 1953.
11. ERIKSON, E. H. *Identity and the Life Cycle.* New York: International Universities Press, 1959.
12. FERENCZI, S. *Thalassa: A Theory of Genitality.* London: Hogarth Press, 1923.
13. ————. *Further Contributions to the Theory and Technique of Psychoanalysis.* London: Hogarth Press, 1926. *Final Contributions,* 1955.
14. FREUD, S. Constructions in Analysis (1937). Analysis Terminable and Interminable (1937). *Standard Edition,* Vol. 23. London: Hogarth Press, 1964.

15. ———. *The Origins of Psychoanalysis; Letters to Wilhelm Fliess* (1887-1902). New York: Basic Books, 1954.
16. Frosch, J., et al. Panel on Severe Regressive States. *Journal of the American Psychoanalytic Association,* Vol. 15, 1967. Also see Panel Reports in Vol. 6, 1958, and Vol. 14, 1966.
17. Furst, S. S. (Ed.). *Psychic Trauma.* New York: Basic Books, 1967. See chapters by S. Furst, L. Rangell, P. Neubauer, P. Greenacre, J. Sandler, A. Solnit, R. Waelder, A. Freud.
18. Greenson, R. R. Empathy and Its Vicissitudes. *International Journal of Psycho-Analysis,* Vol. 41, 1960.
19. ———. The Working Alliance and the Transference Neurosis. *Psychoanalytic Quarterly,* Vol. 34, 1965.
20. Hacker, F. J. The Discriminatory Function of the Ego. *International Journal of Psycho-Analysis,* Vol. 43, 1962.
21. ———. The Reality of Myth. *International Journal of Psycho-Analysis,* Vol. 45, 1964.
22. Hartmann, H. *Ego Psychology and the Problems of Adaptation.* New York: W. W. Norton, 1958.
23. Holt, R. R., et al. Ego Autonomy Re-evaluated. *International Journal of Psychiatry,* Vol. 4, 1967.
24. ——— (Ed.). *Motives and Thought: Psychoanalytic Essays in Honor of David Rapaport. Psychological Issues,* Vol. 5, No. 2-3, 1967.
25. Hoppe, K. D. Relaxation Through Concentration—Concentration Through Relaxation. *Medical Times,* March 1961.
26. Huizinga, J. *Homo Ludens: A Study of the Play-Element in Culture.* Boston: Beacon Press, 1950.
27. Kanzer, M. The Motor Sphere of the Transference. *Psychoanalytic Quarterly,* Vol. 35, 1966.
28. Karusch, A. Working Through. *Psychoanalytic Quarterly,* Vol. 36, 1967.
29. Kepecs, J. G. Theories of Transference Neurosis. *Psychoanalytic Quarterly,* Vol. 35, 1966.
30. Kestenberg, J. S. The Role of Movement Patterns in Development. *Psychoanalytic Quarterly,* Vols. 34 and 36, 1965 and 1967.
31. Klein, M. *Envy and Gratitude.* London: Hogarth Press, 1957.
32. Kris, E., J. Herma, and J. Shor. Freud's Theory of the Dream in American Textbooks. *Journal of Abnormal and Social Psychology,* Vol. 38, 1943.
33. Lerner, B. Dream Function Reconsidered. *Journal of Abnormal Psychology,* Vol. 72, 1967.
34. Lindon, J. A. (Ed.). On Regression: A Workshop. *Psychoanalytic Forum,* Vol. 2, 1967.
35. Loewald, H. W. (Chairman). Activity-Passivity Symposium of American Psychoanalytic Association. *Journal of the American Psychoanalytic Association,* Vol. 15, 1967.
36. Lowen, A. *Physical Dynamics of Character Structure.* New York: Macmillan, 1958.
37. Milner, M. Aspects of Symbolism in the Comprehension of the "Not-Self." *International Journal of Psycho-Analysis,* Vol. 33, 1952.
38. Money-Kyrle, R. E. On the Process of Psychoanalytical Inference. *International Journal of Psycho-Analysis,* Vol. 39, 1958.
39. Pribram, K. The New Neurology: Memory, Novelty, Thought, and Choice. In G. H. Blaser (Ed.), *EEG and Behavior.* New York: Grune & Stratton, 1953.
40. ———. Freud's Project: An Open Biologically Based Model for Psycho-Analysis. In N. S. Greenfield and W. C. Lewis (Eds.), *Psycho-Analysis and Current Biological Thought.* Madison: University of Wisconsin Press, 1965.
41. Rangell, L. Psychoanalysis, Affects, and the "Human Core." *Psychoanalytic Quarterly,* Vol. 36, 1967.
42. ———. A Further Attempt to Resolve the "Problems of Anxiety." *Journal of the American Psychoanalytic Association,* Vol. 16, 1968.

43. Rapaport, D. On the Psychoanalytic Theory of Affects. *International Journal of Psycho-Analysis,* Vol. 34, 1953.
44. Reich, W. *Selected Writings.* New York: W. W. Norton, 1960.
45. Ross, N. The "As If" Concept. *Journal of the American Psychoanalytic Association,* Vol. 15, 1967.
46. Rycroft, C. On Idealization, Illusion, and Catastrophic Disillusion. *International Journal of Psycho-Analysis,* Vol. 36, 1955.
47. Schafer, R. The Clinical Analysis of Affects. *Journal of the American Psychoanalytic Association,* Vol. 12, 1964.
48. Shor, J. A Well-Spring of Psychoanalysis. *Psychoanalysis,* Vol. 2, 1953.
49. ————. Female Sexuality: Aspects and Prospects. *Psychoanalysis,* Vol. 2, 1954.
50. ————. The Ethic of Freud's Psychoanalysis. *International Journal of Psycho-Analysis,* Vol. 42, 1961.
51. ————. Charles Darwin: Grandfather of Modern Psychotherapy. *International Mental Health Research Bulletin,* 1963.
52. ————. Primary Love—Primary Illusion. *Contemporary Psychology,* Vol. 14, 1969.
53. Spitz, R. *No and Yes.* New York: International Universities Press, 1957.
54. Tabachnick, N. Self-Realization and Social Definition. *International Journal of Psycho-Analysis,* Vol. 48, 1967.
55. Waelder, R. Inhibitions, Symptoms, and Anxiety: Forty Years Later. *Psychoanalytic Quarterly,* Vol. 36, 1967.

References

Page numbers in parentheses following each reference indicate where in this book the reference is discussed. (References to the reprinted article in Appendix B are listed separately on pages 177-179.)

Balint, E. (1972) Fair Shares and Mutual Concern *Internat. J. Psychoanalysis.* Vol. 53. Pt. I. (30, 155)

Balint, M. (1932) Character Analysis and New Beginning in *Primary Love and Psycho-Analytic Technique.* New York: Liveright Publishing Corp., 1952. (49, 108)

Balint, M. (1952) *Primary Love and Psycho-Analytic Technique.* New York: Liveright Publishing Corp., 1952 (24-26, 49, 63, 65)

Balint, M. (1959) *Thrills and Regressions.* New York: International Universities Press, 1959. (24-26, 29, 49, 63, 65, 108, 130, 146)

Balint, M. (1968) *The Basic Fault.* London: Hogarth Press, 1968. (12, 49, 63, 65, 106, 125)

Bardwick, E. (1974) The Sex Hormones, the Central Nervous System, and Affect Variability in Humans, in *Women in Therapy: New Psychotherapies for a Changing Society* (Edit. V. Franks and V. Burtle). New York: Brunner/Mazel Inc., 1974. (29)

Bergler, E. (1949) Did Freud Really Advocate a Hands-Off Policy Towards Artistic Creativity?—*American Imago* Vol. 6, No. 3. (19)

Bion, W.R. (1970) *Attention and Interpretation.* New York: Basic Books, Inc., 1970. (49)-

Blos, P. (1962) *On Adolescence.* New York: The Free Press of Glencoe, Inc. (151, 154)

Bornstein, B. (1951) On Latency, *Psychoanalytic Study of the Child.* Vol. VI. New York: International Universities Press. (142)

Buber, M. (1937) *I and Thou.* New York: Charles Scribner & Sons. 1970. (110-111)

Coleman, M. and Shor, J. (1953) Ego Development Through Self-Traumatization, *Psychoanalytic Review*, Vol. XL, No. 3. (127)

Darwin, C. (1871) *The Descent of Man.* New York: Modern Library (G 27). (15, 17, 125)

Darwin, C. (1872) *The Expression of the Emotions in Man and Animals.* New York: Modern Library (G 27). (16, 18, 108)

Deutsch, H. (1945) *The Psychology of Women*, Vol. 1. New York: Grune & Stratton. (151)

Erikson, E. (1950) *Childhood and Society*. New York: W.W. Norton & Co., Inc. 1963. (23, 111)

Erikson, E. (1964) *Insight and Responsibility*. New York: W.W. Norton & Co. Inc. 1964. (24, 111)

Escalona, S.K. and Leitch, M. (1949) The Reactions of Infants to Stress. In *The Psychoanalytic Study of the Child.* New York International University Press. (142)

Escalona, S.K. and Leitch, M. et al. (1953) Early Phases of Personality Development. Monographs of the Society for Research in Child Development, Vol. XVII, Serial No. 54. No. 1. (142)

Escalona, S. (1968) *The Roots of Individuality*. Chicago: Aldine Pub. Co. (26, 142)

Fenichel, O. (1945) *The Psychoanalytic Theory of the Neurosis.* New York: W.W. Norton & Co., Inc. 1945. (14, 23)

Ferenczi, S. (1923) *Thalassa: A Theory of Genitality*. New York: The Psychoanalytic Quarterly, Inc., 1938. (20)

Ferenczi, S. (1926) *Theory and Technique of Psycho-Analysis.* London: Hogarth Press, 1969. (62, 125, 131-132)

Ferenczi, S. (1929) The Principles of Relaxation and Neocatharsis, in *Problems and Methods of Psycho-Analysis.* New York: Basic Books, 1955. (62-63)

Freud, S. (1895) Studies in Hysteria: Frau Emmy Von N., in *Standard Edition* Vol. II. London: Hogarth Press. (44, 51, 125)

Freud, S. (1905) Three Contributions to a Theory of Sexuality, in *Standard Edition*, Vol. VII. (17, 76, 108)

Freud, S. (1908) "Civilized" Sexual Morality and Modern Nervous Illness, in *Standard Edition*, Vol. IX. (4)

Freud, S. (1914) On The History of the Psycho-Analytic Movement, in *Standard Edition*, Vol. XIV. (6, 122)

Freud, S. (1914a) Remembering, Repeating and Working-through (Further Recommendations on the Technique of Psycho-Analysis II), in *Standard Edition*, Vol. XII. (5, 6)

Freud, S. (1914b) Observations on Transference Love, in *Standard Edition*, Vol. XII. (61)

Freud, S. (1920) Beyond the Pleasure Principle, in *Standard Edition*, Vol. XVIII. (130-131)

Freud, S. (1923) The Ego and the Id, in *Standard Edition*, Vol. XIX. (19, 23, 129, 150)

Freud, S. (1927) The Future of an Illusion, in *Standard Edition*, Vol. XXI. (5)

Freud, S. (1931) Female Sexuality, in *Standard Edition*, Vol. XXI. (6, 143, 146-149, 153-154)

Freud, S. (1932) Femininity, in *Standard Edition*, Vol. XXII. (6, 144)

Freud, S. (1937) Analysis Terminable and Interminable, in *Standard Edition*, Vol. XXIII. (100)

Freud, S. (1937a) Constructions in Analysis, in *Standard Edition*, Vol. XXIII. (123)

Freud, S. (1938) Splitting of the Ego in the Process of Defense, in *Standard Edition*, Vol. XXIII. (29, 130)

Freud, S. (1939) Outline of Psycho-analysis, in *Standard Edition*, Vol. XXIII. (61)

Fromm, E. (1956) *The Art of Loving*. New York: Harper & Brothers. (22)

Galenson, E. and Roiphe, H. (1972) The Impact of Early Sexual Discovery on Mood, Defensive Organization, and Symbolization, in *Psychoan. Study of the Child.* New York: International Universities Press. (142)

Greenacre, P. (1966). Discussion "On Weeping." *Internat. J. Psychoanalysis*, Vol. 47. (109)-

Greenacre, P. (1971) Clinical Studies of Development, in *Emotional Growth*, Vol. I. New York: International Universities Press. (29, 142, 145)

Harrington, A. (1971) The Coming of the Psychopath, in *Playboy Magazine*, Dec. 1971. (1, 22, 31)

Heard, G. (1963) *Five Ages of Man—The Psychology of Human History*. New York: Julian Press. (112)

Huizinga, J. (1944) *Homo Ludens: A Study of the Play-Element in Culture*. Boston: Beacon Press. 1950. (20)

Kardener, S., Fuller, M., and Mensh, I., (1973) A Survey of Physicians' Attitudes and Practices Regarding Erotic and Non-erotic Contacts With Patients, in *J. American Psychiatric Association*, Vol. 130 #10. (61)

Keniston, K. (1970) Youth, A "New" Stage of Life, *The American Scholar*, Vol. 39. No. 4. (112)

Kernberg, O. (1975) *Borderline Conditions and Pathological Narcissism*. New York: Jason Aronson, Inc. (125)

Kesterberg, J.S. (1975) *Children and Parents: Psychoanalytic Studies in Development*. New York: Jason Aronson, Inc. (142)

Kinsey, et al. (1953) *Sexual Behavior in the Human Female*. Phila. and London: W.B. Saunders. 1953 (134)

Klein, M. (1957) Envy and Gratitude, in *Intern. Psycho-Analytical Library* No. 104, London: Hogarth Press. (25, 28, 96, 108, 142, 149)

Kohut, H. (1971) *The Analysis of the Self*. New York: International Universities Press, Inc. (64-65, 108, 130, 156)

Kohut, H. (1977) *The Restoration of the Self*. New York: International Universities Press, Inc. (125)

Kris, E. (1952) *Psychoanalytic Explorations in Art*. New York: International Universities Press. (130)

Kris, E. (1954) Introduction to *The Origins of Psycho-Analysis:* Freud's Letters to W. Fliess, Drafts, Notes: 1887-1902. New York: Basic Books, Inc., 1954. (16, 17, 19)

Kris, E., Herma, H. and Shor, J. (1943) Freud's Theory of the Dream in American Textbooks, in *Journal of Abnormal and Social Psychology*, Vol. 38, No. 3. (139)

Luce, G.G. (1970) *Biological Rhythms in Psychiatry and Medicine*. National Institute of Mental Health. Public Health Service Publication No. 2088, 1970. (112)

Mahler, M. (1975) *The Psychological Birth of the Human Infant*. New York: Basic Books, Inc. (142)

Milner, M. (1950) *On Not Being Able to Paint*. London: Heinemann Educational Books Ltd., 1971. (49)

Milner, M. (1955) The Role of Illusion in Symbol Formation, in *New Directions in Psycho-Analysis*. Ne York: Basic Books, 1955. (21, 49)

Milner, M. (1969) *The Hands of the Living God*. New York: International Universities Press. (49)

Mitchell, G.D. (1968) Attachment Differences in Male and Female Infant Monkeys, in *Child Development*, Vol. 39.(2). (144)

Morgan, E. (1972) *The Descent of Woman*. New York: Stein and Day. (15, 141)

Olsen, P. (Editor) (1975) *Emotional Floodings*. New York: Basic Books. (10, 16, 31)

Parsons, T. (1951) *The Social Systems*. The Free Press, Glencoe, Illinois. (43)

Reik, T. (1937) *Surprise and the Psycho-Analyst—On the Conjecture and Comprehension of Unconscious Processes*. New York: E.P. Dutton and Co. (19, 20, 49-50)

Rubenstein, B. and Levitt, M. (1973) Therapeutic Systems and Moral Assumptions. Presented at the Los Angeles Psychoanalytic Society, January, 1973. (61-62)

Sanville, J. (1968) Cultural Traditions as Codeterminants of Goal Setting, in *The Course of Human Life*, (Edit. C. Buhler). New York: Springer Publishing Co. Inc., 1968. (141-142)

Sanville, J. (1975) Therapists in Competition and Cooperation with Exorcists: The Spirit World Revisited, in *Clinical Social Work Journal*, Vol. 3, No. 4, 1975. (144-147)

Sanville, J. (1975a) Dreaming as Playing. Paper presented at the Los Angeles Conference of Div. of Psychotherapy, A.P.A., Dec. 1975. (20)

Sanville, J. (1976) Dreaming as Playing: A Clinical Approach. Seminar at the Institute of Clinical Social Work. Jan. 1976. (20)

Sanville, J. and Shor, J. (1973) Leading Ladies and Gentle Men, in *Clinical Social Work Journal,* Vol. 1, No. 2, 1973. (15, 43, 65, 93)

Sanville, J. and Shor, J. (1975) Women in Transcendence, in *Clinical Social Work Journal,* Vol. 3, No. 1, 1975. (16, 17)-

Sanville, J. and Shor, J. (1975a) Age Games in Playmating, in *Clinical Social Work Journal,* Vol. 3, No. 4, 1975. (76-93)

Sanville, J. and Shor, J. (1975b) Four Further Freedoms—Mental Health Values beyond Abundance. Presented at World Federation of Mental Health Conference. Copenhagen, Aug. 1975. (136)

Sanville, J. and Shor, J. (1976) Spontaneous Surrogates and Shifting Chauvinisms. Presented at U.C.L.A. Conference on Legal and Professional Issues in Sex Therapy and the Use of Sex Surrogates. May, 1976. (102)

Schafer, R. (1968) *Aspects of Internalization.* New York: International Universities Press. (92)

Shepard, M. (1971) *The Love Treatment: Sexual Intimacy between Patients and Psychotherapists.* New York: Weyden Press. (61)

Shor, J. (1939) Moreno's Sociometry—An Experiment in Individualism, in *Journal of Social Studies,* Vol. I, No. 1, 1939. (22-23)

Shor, J. (1953) A Well-Spring of Psychoanalysis, in *Psychoanalysis—Journal of Psychoanalytic Psychology,* Vol. 2, No. 1, 1953. (126)

Shor, J. (1954) Female Sexuality—Aspects and Prospects, in *Psychoanalysis—Journal of Psychoanalytic Psychology,* Vol. 2, No. 3, Winter 1954. (27-28, 114, 133)

Shor, J. (1961) The Ethic of Freud's Psycho-Analysis, in *Internat. Journal of Psychoanalysis,* Vol. XLII, Part I-II, 1961. (68)

Shor, J. (1962) Sources for Psycho-analysis in the Writings of Charles Darwin, presented at Imago Society, London, Nov. 1962. (16, 19)

Shor, J. (1963) Self-Provocation and Reparation. Paper presented to the British Psycho-Analytic Society, February 1963. (16, 19, 126)

Shor, J. (1963a) Charles Darwin—Grandfather of Modern Psychotherapy, in *Internat. Mental Health Research Newsletter,* Vol. V, Spring, 1963. (19)

Shor, J. (1969) Primary Love—Primary Illusion, in *Contemporary Psychology,* Vol. 14, No. 7, 1969. (106)

Shor, J. (1970) Human Male or Human Being? in *Psychiatry and Social Science Review,* January 1970. (52, 156)

Shor, J. (1972) Two Principles of Reparative Regression: Self-traumatization and Self-provocation, in *Psychoanalytic Review,* Vol. 59, No. 2, 1972. (19, 26, 63, 70, 74, 92, 153)

Shor, J. (1977) Two Biases in Psychotherapeutic Practice. Paper presented to the L.A. Society of Clinical Psychologists, June 1977. (11, 46)

Shor, J. and Sanvile, J. (1974) Erotic Provocations and Dalliances in Psychotherapeutic Practice, in *Clinical Social Work Journal,* Vol. 2, No. 3, 1974. (60-75)

Spitz, R.A. (1945) Hospitalism: an inquiry into the genesis of psychiatric conditions in early childhood. *Psychoanalytic Study of the Child,* Vol. I, New York: International Universities Press. (28)

Spitz, R.A. and Wolf, K.M. (1949) Autoeroticism: some empirical Findings and hypotheses on three of its manifestations in the first year of life. *Psychoan. Study of the Child.* New York: International Universities Press. (143)

Swartz, J. et al. (1969) The Erotized Transference and other Transference Problems, in *Psychoanalytic Forum,* Vol. 3. (61)

Walters, P.A., (1965) Promiscuity in Adolescence, *American Journal of Orthopsychiatry,* Vol. XXV, No. 4. (152)

Winnicott, D.W. (1965) *The Maturational Processes and the Facilitating Environment.* New York: International Universities Press. (49)

Winnicott, D.W. (1971) *Playing and Reality.* New York: Basic Books, Inc., 1971. (20, 21, 48-49, 91, 125)

Index of Subjects

Illusion in Loving was designed and produced by
Project Publishing & Design in Santa Monica, California.
The book is set by direct entry photocomposition in Caledonia,
a typeface designed by W.A. Dwiggins in 1938
to be both distinctive and readable.
Malloy Lithographing, Inc., of Ann Arbor, Michigan
printed the book on 60-pound Glatfelter Offset paper
with a regular finish.